Getting Up
and Down

Getting Up and Down

How to Save Strokes from Forty Yards and In

Tom Watson with Nick Seitz

Illustration by Anthony Ravielli
Introduction by Jack Nicklaus

HODDER AND STOUGHTON
LONDON SYDNEY AUCKLAND

British Library Cataloguing in Publication Data

Watson, Tom, 1949–
    Getting up and down
    1. Golf
    I. Title   II. Seitz, Nick
    796.352′3   GV965

    ISBN 0-340-40192-3

First published in Great Britain 1984. This edition 1992.
Reproduced from the original setting by arrangement with
Random House, Inc., New York.

Published by Hodder and Stoughton, a division of Hodder and
Stoughton Ltd, Mill Road, Dunton Green, Sevenoaks, Kent TN13 2YE.
Editorial Office: 47 Bedford Square, London, WC1B 3DP.

Printed in Great Britain by
BPCC Hazells Ltd
Member of BPCC Ltd

This book is dedicated to my mother and father, Sallie Bet and Hook, and to my wife, Linda, without whose inspiration, teaching and love, my dreams would never have been realized.

Contents

Introduction by Jack Nicklaus

The cover photograph on this book says it all about Tom Watson's short game. I felt I'd played well enough to win the 1982 U.S. Open at Pebble Beach, and when Tom hit his tee shot on the 17th hole into the rough near the flagstick I thought there was no way he could get up and down in two. He didn't get up and down, of course—he holed it.

That wasn't the first time he did it to me in a major championship with his short game. In the 1977 British Open at Turnberry, I shot 65–66 the final two rounds and lost to his 65–65. I thought I had him the last day until he holed a putt of at least fifty feet from the fringe on 15.

Those were great scoring shots, and Tom's strongest weapon is his ability to score. He knows the only thing that really matters is the total number at the bottom of the scorecard every day. And he knows you *score* with the short game.

Tom's one of the finest putters I've ever seen, and the secret to me is that he knows he isn't going to miss many short putts, so he can be aggressive and take a run at a long putt or chip. Someday maybe he'll start missing some short putts and come back into the real world, but in the meantime his short game makes him awfully hard to beat.

In sum, Tom's scoring ability is superlative. His method is simple, aggressive and very firm, he's always accelerating the clubhead through the ball, he's a wonderful concentrator, and I've rarely seen anyone who approaches the short shots with more confidence.

Those are all great qualities, and I commend to you both Tom's short-game mechanics and his attitude.

Preface by Nick Seitz

Less than twenty-four hours after Thomas Sturges Watson won his fifth British Open, he was working intensely on this book with me and artist Tony Ravielli in the Connecticut home of Random House Managing Editor Tony Wimpfheimer. Give British Airways and its Concorde an assist in the publishing credits.

Does a superstar like Watson *really* get involved in the instruction that appears under his byline? As editorial director of *Golf Digest*, where this material first began to appear, I am asked that question all too often, and I can assure you that Watson said everything that appears here—and went over it and the accompanying artwork at least three times, changing, clarifying and emphasizing until he was satisfied.

He devoted a full hour to rewording, in proof form, his unusual theory of the left elbow in the putting stroke that appears on pages 28 and 29. "Let's get it right," he must have said at least a hundred times over the year we worked on this book, whenever energies threatened to flag.

One day toward the end, we spent eight hours in the Kansas City law office of his manager and brother-in-law Charles Rubin, who played a key role by catering great masses of barbecue from the legendary Arthur Bryant's restaurant (Calvin Trillin calls it the finest barbecue place in the country, and I am not prepared to dispute him). Then we met after dinner at my hotel to finish the chapters on sand play.

Unfortunately, the hotel was hit by a power outage thirty minutes into our session. Watson was not to be deterred. As others left our floor, we continued in a hallway under a weak emergency light. We were making acceptable progress until smoke and fire forced a full evacuation of the hotel. After we knocked on neighboring doors to be sure everyone was out, Watson led the way several stories down a dark stairwell and we repaired to his kitchen, where we continued until midnight.

In my experience, the better the player, the more of a perfectionist he is about his magazine articles and books. This attitude is one reason that Jack Nicklaus and Tom Watson are great players.

Watson was the major influence in the selection of the theme for the book (which evolved long before he chipped in on the 17th at Pebble Beach) and then in the formulation of the format. He and I both wanted a simple, graphic book that would help people score better the easiest way they can: through quick tips on the short game. You and I may not be able to swing a driver like Tom Watson, but we can learn much from the logic and technique of his short game, which is predicted on a clear-minded, spin-free approach that takes the complexity and inconsistency out of recovery play.

The book is organized and designed not only for easy assimilation the first time through, but for quick reference thereafter. If you're having trouble with the short pitch shot over a hazard, you can readily find that section of the book and refresh yourself on how to play it.

We began all this by taping twenty-five hours of material, which was then transcribed by Jan Costello and Sharan Smith of *Golf Digest*. Their bigger job was reading and retyping our hand-scrawled editing of the copy, some of which went back and forth three and four times.

Also deserving of thanks are *Golf Digest* editors Larry Dennis and Jerry Tarde, and Andy Nusbaum, director of Golf Digest Instruction Schools, who were always available to read and react to our work-in-progress. Dorothy Geiser, who designed the book, was resourceful throughout. A health maven, she suffered magnificently the inveterate pipe smoking of Tony Ravielli and myself.

Finally I should thank, for her patience and support, my wife, Velma, a tennis player herself. She gave up her dining-room table to the enterprise, and in fact renamed it The Watson-Book Table.

My lasting memory of the book—and perhaps its ultimate testimonial—derives from a fun round with Watson and a group of mutual friends at the Greenbrier resort in West Virginia. On the last hole, with a crowd gathered around the green, Watson chipped from 65 feet and left the ball a foot from the hole. From about the same distance, with a worse lie in the rough, I chipped inside his ball. I had, as Jerry Pate puts it on tour, "done a Watson." That's when I knew this book had a future.

12

Foreword by Tom Watson

My earliest memory of the game of golf, which is now my profession, was when I was the ripe old age of six. On a hot summer evening the whole Watson family, putters and golf balls in hand, arrived at the practice putting green of the Kansas City Country Club. I will never forget the excitement of that evening, since it was the first time my father allowed me to actually "play" on the course. Using a cut-down putter, my father taught me how to hold it and then simply told me to hit the ball in the hole. This, my first real golfing experience, hooked me on the game forever, because it was fun and a new challenge. Little did I dream then of where golf would take me. And little did I know that that first lesson from my dad was the most important lesson of golf: hit the ball into the hole.

My dad taught me the full golf swing shortly after that, but whenever I had the choice to hit full shots or putt on the putting green, I always chose the old cut-down putter over the old cut-down 5-iron. Trying to solve the problems of the different speeds of breaking putts became my obsession, and whenever possible I spent all my time on the green. I think that my early learning and enthusiasm for putting is the main reason I developed a very good feel for the short game in later years.

The reasons this book deals only with the short game—putting, chipping, pitching and bunker play—are twofold. The first reason is that more than half of all the golf shots we perform on the course are within forty yards of the green. I will use a PGA Tour statistic to prove how important the short game is in relation to the long game. Per round the average pro hits less than thirteen greens in regulation (that is, being on the green with two putts to make par). This means that even a touring professional has to scramble, has to get up and down, on at least five holes out of eighteen. So you see that even these players, who from tee to green are exceptional, rely much of the time on their chipping, pitching, sand play and putting to make their living.

Go to any professional golf tournament and you will see as much practice on and around the practice greens as on the driving range. I venture to say you will not see most amateur golfers spend the same amount of time practicing the short game. It's a shame that these golfers don't recognize the great importance of their short game in reducing their scores.

The second reason I deal only with the short game is that I believe the natural, logical, and easiest way to teach golf is to start with the shortest swing and then increase it to a full swing. I strongly believe it's much easier to learn golf's basic elements—aiming the clubface and hitting the ball consistently in the middle of the clubface—by using a short rather than a long swing.

The fact is that most beginning golfers simply do not have much feel for the speed or distance of a ball hit to a green or rolled over its surface. This book provides several basic practice drills for putting and chipping, from which you can ''learn'' feel and take it with you onto the golf course.

Probably the one shot in my golfing career that will be most remembered was a short but very difficult downhill chip shot on the par 3 71st hole of the 1982 U.S. Open at Pebble Beach. I was tied with Jack Nicklaus and staring a bogey in the face with only one hole left to play. Playing the shot with an open clubface, I hit it just onto the green and watched it break to the right, hit the flagstick dead center, and drop in the hole for a birdie two and a one-shot lead. I birdied the last hole as well, but won my first U.S. Open championship thanks to that chip shot and a little luck.

This book will describe exactly how I hit that chip shot and a great variety of other specialty chip, pitch, and bunker shots. Using no tricks but a lot of common sense, you will learn a logical way to hit almost every type of short shot.

Just to learn the correct stances and techniques by reading this book is not enough. You must practice these various shots to develop feel ''feedback,'' which will greatly improve your chances for success on the course. By learning how to get the ball up and down, you will have mastered the art of scoring your best.

Lastly, without the help of my friends C. A. ''Tony'' Wimpfheimer, Nick Seitz and Tony Ravielli, and of the book's designer Dorothy Geiser, this book would not have been published. My thanks to them all.

Putting

The Basic Putting Stroke

According to a recent study, putting accounts for 43 percent of all shots golfers play. I'd say that's conservative. There's never been any doubt in any professional's mind about the significance of putting. Overheard in tournament locker rooms is the lament "I never make a putt!" We work on putting as much as we do the full swing—after all, if putting is half the game, it deserves half your practice time.

But how many weekend players do you know who expend that kind of effort on putting? How many do you know who've ever taken a putting lesson?

Putting gets major attention in this book because it's a major reason for my success—and for any good player's success. There are no bad putters at the top of the game, and you can bet that the players who are winning on the tour from week to week are putting well. The great players, from Vardon to Nicklaus, invariably have been great putters.

Putting is really a game within a game.

Everything you do on the greens must be more precise and repeatable than it is for your other shotmaking because there's less margin for error. I'm going to give you a physical and mental approach to putting that will clear your mind and allow you to make firm, reliable strokes under pressure and thus consistent contact, so you can predict what the ball will do under different conditions.

I'm known as an aggressive putter, and basically I am. A putt cannot go in the hole if it's short, and I'd rather face a four-footer coming back than leave the ball on the front lip. But I don't always charge a putt. Later, I'll discuss when to be bold and when not to be. First, though, the basics.

Putting is mostly feel and touch and judging distance. Throw in good mechanics and you are a good putter. In this chapter I'm going to discuss the two principal parts of putting: how to learn mechanics and how to learn feel. Mechanics is 10 percent of it, feel 90 percent. Mechanics is the easy part, feel the more difficult to learn. But good mechanics lead to good feel.

I'm going to talk about the crucial keys of acceleration and contacting the ball on the sweet spot. By acceleration I mean the putterhead must be gaining speed rather than losing it at impact. And a solid hit is achieved not only by striking the back of the ball squarely but also by striking it with the most solid portion of the putterface, and striking it firmly. I'm going to talk about a common yet little discussed fault of bad putters concerning the angle of the left elbow at address and its position during the backswing and follow-through. I'm going to talk about the grip and setup.

But always bear in mind that putting is the most individualistic part of the golf game. There are all kinds of different styles, many more than with the full golf swing. The stroke is so short it allows for mechanical variations. But there are certain fundamentals all great putters share, and we must deal with them.

After we put together the mechanics of a sound stroke, I'll give you some exercises to ingrain them and also to learn the most important part of putting—feel, touch, a sense of distance. I think you will be a better putter when we finish. And that means you'll be a *much* better player.

The putting stroke

In the pages that follow I'll tell and show you how I make a controlled, rhythmic, repeating stroke. I'll talk about, among other points, how to set up and aim, how to contain your backswing, and how to accelerate the putter through the ball for solid contact. I'll show you why I consider a consistent bend of the left elbow absolutely critical.

As you can see, I putt with my arms and shoulders, keeping my wrists firm throughout the stroke, the left hand guiding the stroke back and through. Only on exceptionally long putts will there be some breaking of the wrists going back and coming through.

My head stays still until one count after impact. The one reason most putts are missed is the head looks up too soon. By counting to one after impact before looking up, you assure the continuation of the stroke.

It's important, by the way, not to follow the putter back with your eyes. You must maintain eye contact with the ball to hit it solidly. If your eyes follow the putterhead, they must flick back to the ball before the putter gets there, causing inconsistent hits and a stroke that gets too quick.

Now let's take the stroke apart—then put it back together again.

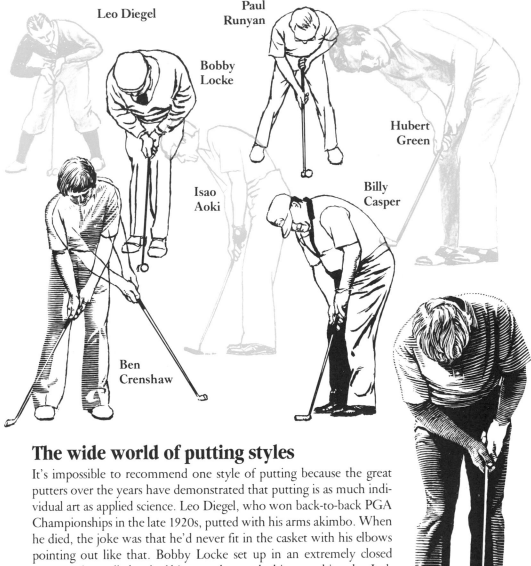

Leo Diegel
Paul Runyan
Bobby Locke
Hubert Green
Isao Aoki
Billy Casper
Ben Crenshaw
Jack Nicklaus

The wide world of putting styles

It's impossible to recommend one style of putting because the great putters over the years have demonstrated that putting is as much individual art as applied science. Leo Diegel, who won back-to-back PGA Championships in the late 1920s, putted with his arms akimbo. When he died, the joke was that he'd never fit in the casket with his elbows pointing out like that. Bobby Locke set up in an extremely closed stance and actually hooked his putts the way he hit everything else. Jack Nicklaus, on the other hand, sets up open. Isao Aoki of Japan addresses the ball with the toe of the putter up in the air, picks the putter up wristily and hits down on the ball. Paul Runyan has been known to separate his hands widely on the club, and Sam Snead goes sidesaddle in his senior years. Hubert Green bends low over the ball, but Don January stands virtually straight up. Billy Casper "pops" the ball with a little jab of a stroke, while Ben Crenshaw makes a long, flowing stroke with his hands and arms. These diverse styles have one thing in common: they all work.

How I set up to putt

Putting styles vary so much because putting is a matter of comfort and because the stroke is short and requires no lower-body movement—all you need is a stable address position. I bend from the hips so my arms can hang freely, the elbows resting close to my sides. I like to keep my weight centered—if anything, it should favor the left side—and I position the ball just forward of the center of my stance. The stance should be at least shoulder width for good balance—be careful not to let it get too narrow. I stand slightly open to feel I go out and down the line with my right hand and arm.

My hands are slightly ahead of the ball and in a *bowed position*, which keeps them locked with the forearms throughout the stroke. This locked position eliminates excess wrist movement and forces you to move the putter with your arms. Under pressure I believe this is better than a wristy stroke, and produces an accelerating action.

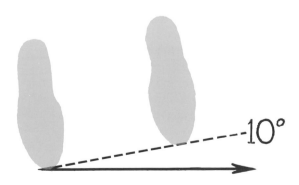

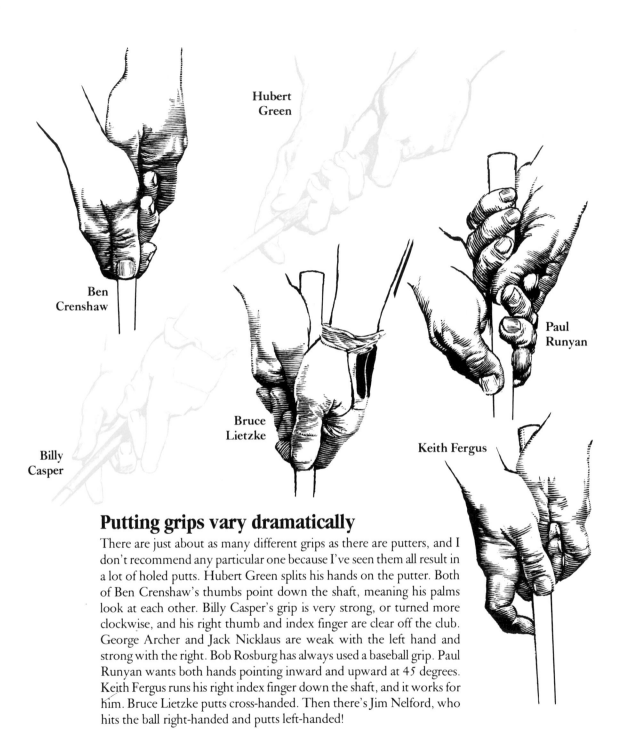

Hubert
Green

Ben
Crenshaw

Billy
Casper

Bruce
Lietzke

Paul
Runyan

Keith Fergus

Putting grips vary dramatically

There are just about as many different grips as there are putters, and I
don't recommend any particular one because I've seen them all result in
a lot of holed putts. Hubert Green splits his hands on the putter. Both
of Ben Crenshaw's thumbs point down the shaft, meaning his palms
look at each other. Billy Casper's grip is very strong, or turned more
clockwise, and his right thumb and index finger are clear off the club.
George Archer and Jack Nicklaus are weak with the left hand and
strong with the right. Bob Rosburg has always used a baseball grip. Paul
Runyan wants both hands pointing inward and upward at 45 degrees.
Keith Fergus runs his right index finger down the shaft, and it works for
him. Bruce Lietzke putts cross-handed. Then there's Jim Nelford, who
hits the ball right-handed and putts left-handed!

22

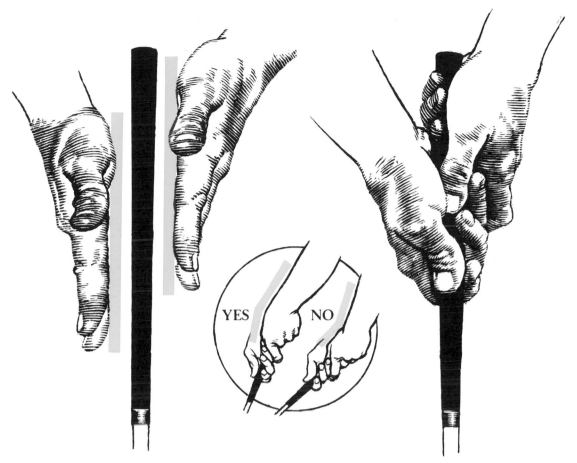

YES   NO

Why I use a palms-facing grip

No one grip is exactly right for every golfer, but every golfer has one grip that fits him or her. I personally use a palms-facing grip: both palms facing each other squarely with the thumbs pointing down the top of the grip. The back of my left hand faces the line of the putt.

My putting grip is a reverse overlap, with the index finger of the left hand resting on the crevice between the last two fingers of the right hand. You can use any grip you feel comfortable with, but I prefer that the palms always face each other so the hands can work in unison. I think this grip is reliable with any sort of stroke. My grip is neutral—neither strong nor weak. At address, most of my grip pressure is in my left hand so I can guide the stroke with that hand. Specifically, my grip pressure is primarily in the last three fingers of the left hand and the index and middle two fingers of the right hand.

I sole the putter very lightly, not even permitting the weight of the club to rest on the ground. Otherwise the grass can catch the putter on the takeaway and ruin the path of the stroke.

Find your putter's sweet spot...

Every putter has its solid point, or sweet spot, and it can vary from one model to the next. By contacting the ball consistently on the sweet spot, your feel for the distance the ball rolls will improve. To find it, simply dangle the putter between your thumb and forefinger, gripping lightly and letting it hang freely. Then with your other forefinger tap at various spots along the blade until the putterhead rebounds *straight back*. The blade shouldn't flutter or twist. The point on the putter-face at which the head rebounds straight back is the sweet spot.

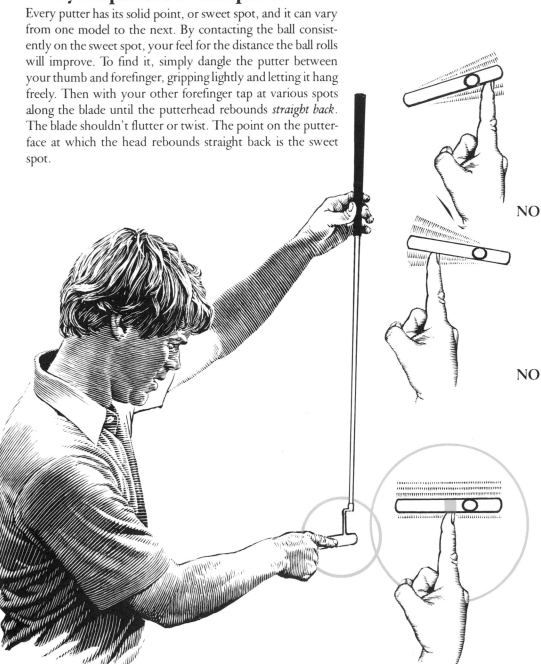

NO

NO

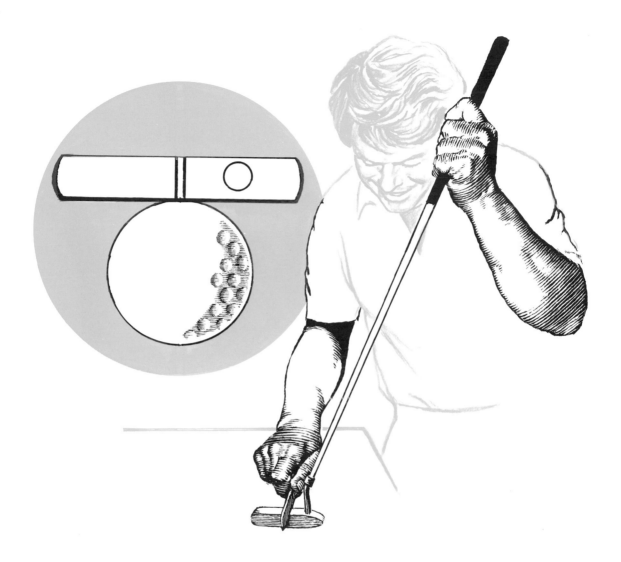

...then mark and apply it

Once you've found the sweet spot, mark it on the top of the putter with a little notch or spot of paint or piece of tape. (Your putter may carry an alignment line that has nothing to do with the location of the sweet spot.) When you address a putt, place the sweet spot directly behind the ball and square to your target. You want to contact the ball right on that sweet spot. My very last thought before I begin the stroke is always to hit the ball with the sweet spot.

Aim the putter, then align your body

I follow a definite pattern in making my final approach to a putt and taking aim, which is absolutely critical to accurate putting. It's essentially the same procedure I'd follow in aiming a gun. My last look at the line is from behind the ball. Having made up my mind about the line, I move up next to the ball and make two practice swings, as close to the real stroke as I can make them. I'm concentrating on getting a feel for the speed of the putt, the most important factor.

In this illustration of a straight putt, I use my normal open stance to make these practice strokes *parallel* to the line (left of it) because I want to avoid the tendency to move into the ball and aim to the right—if you aim your practice strokes at the hole, that same putter position and body alignment will aim the ball to the right of the hole once you set up to the ball.

Aim the putter, then align your body accordingly. Too many people align the body first, which invariably causes faulty aiming. Consistent, accurate aiming comes from practice, and becomes instinctive if you follow this routine.

Eyes over the ball and square

Setting up to a putt, make sure both eyes are on the target line directly over the ball, or over the target line slightly behind the ball. Some good putters position their eyes *looking out* at the ball, but I've rarely seen a good putter who is *looking in* at the ball.

If your eyes are set looking in, you will tend to pull your putts; if your eyes are looking out, you will tend to push your putts. To test yourself, set up to a putt and drop a second ball from between your eyes. It should land on the ball you're addressing or on the target line behind it.

Be sure your eyes are parallel to the target line—not cocked left or right.

Swivel your head, don't lift it

With a good head position and eye line established, don't cause an unnecessary problem when you look at your target before you stroke the ball. Many golfers lift, rather than swivel, their heads to take a last look or two at the target—and lose their eye line. Usually they end up with their eyes aligned out to the right, and that's where the stroke and the ball go.

Even tour players have problems with eye alignment—as good a player as Lanny Wadkins, for one, tends to look to the right and then push his putts or else overcompensate and pull them. Maintain your eye line by swiveling your head back and forth to look at the target. You'll see the line of the putt and you'll be less prone to look up too soon.

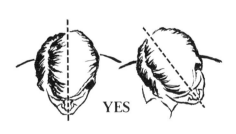

YES

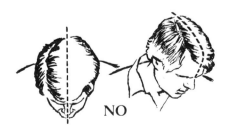

NO

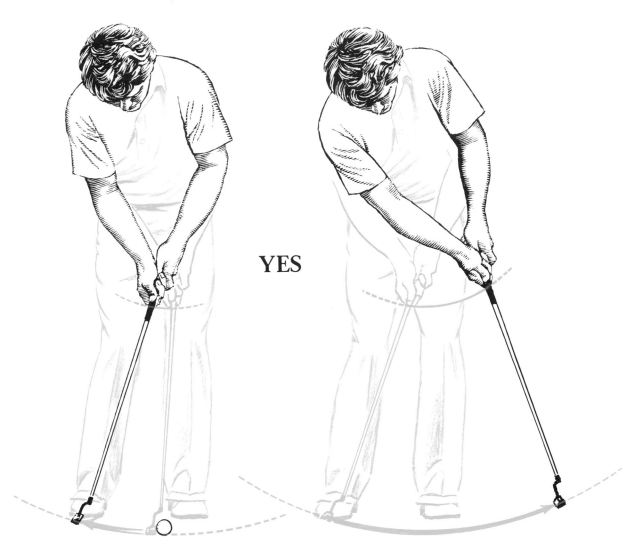

YES

Keep the bend of the left elbow consistent

We come now to a major, major point. This is probably the most important mechanical element in putting, and yet almost no one mentions it. The angle of the left elbow remains constant throughout the stroke, eliminating unnecessary extending and retracting of the arm. If I keep the angle of the left elbow constant, *my shoulders must move as a unit with my arms*, providing a consistent guide for the stroke and producing a perfect arc time after time, like a pendulum.

You don't want extension and retraction, and the next page shows why. My key thought for the stroke is to keep the angle of my left elbow the same so I don't break down.

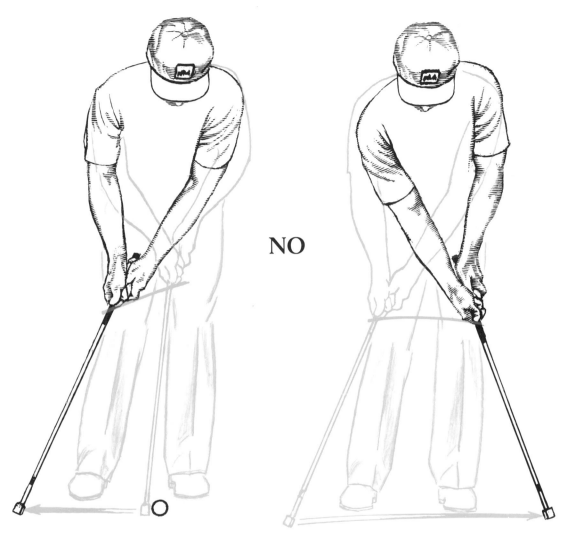

NO

If the left elbow extends, compensations must follow

If you extend your left elbow on the backswing, you must retract it on the forward swing or else hit the ground behind the ball. I think this is the most common mechanical fault in putting.

The left arm often extends because of an excessive effort to keep the putterhead too close to the ground. Telling people to keep the putter low to the ground can be bad advice, causing mis-hit and misdirected putts. If you have this problem, the feeling is that the movement of your arms has become disconnected from the movement of your shoulders.

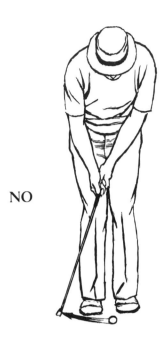

NO

To accelerate the putter, swing it back shorter . . .

Most putting problems are caused by deceleration at impact. The putter wavers and moves off line. To counter this tendency, I try to make sure the putterhead is accelerating—gaining speed—as it swings into and through the ball.

Mechanically I determine how far I will hit a particular putt by the length of my backswing. Of course there are many variables: the speed of the green, the grain, whether the putt is uphill or downhill. You need to find the length of backswing that will produce an accelerating stroke and propel the ball a certain distance on a given putting surface. On very fast greens—Oakmont's, for example—I'll make my stroke shorter than usual, with the same rhythm.

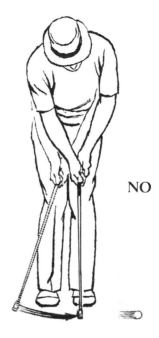

NO

...than you take it through

Most poor putters take the putter back too far and then decelerate coming into the ball. Bob Hope is a prime offender. I've worked with him, but haven't been able to get him to shorten his backswing and make a more forceful stroke. He's done pretty well with his method, but I can see why Bing beat him more times than he beat Bing.

Having contained the length of my backswing, I accelerate the putter into and through the ball, giving the ball a solid, authoritative rap. My contact will be much more consistent, even if I mis-hit the ball. This is one of my important keys for good putting: to accelerate the putter through the ball.

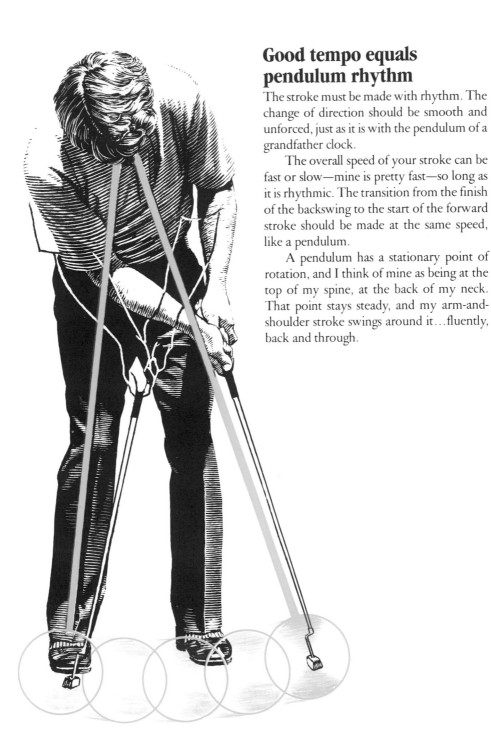

Good tempo equals pendulum rhythm

The stroke must be made with rhythm. The change of direction should be smooth and unforced, just as it is with the pendulum of a grandfather clock.

The overall speed of your stroke can be fast or slow—mine is pretty fast—so long as it is rhythmic. The transition from the finish of the backswing to the start of the forward stroke should be made at the same speed, like a pendulum.

A pendulum has a stationary point of rotation, and I think of mine as being at the top of my spine, at the back of my neck. That point stays steady, and my arm-and-shoulder stroke swings around it...fluently, back and through.

As Sam Snead says, listen for the ball to drop

Every golfer gets anxious and looks up too soon now and then. A good way to keep from looking up is to listen for the ball to go into the hole. That's one of Sam Snead's old favorites. He doesn't look up until—hopefully—he hears the ball rattle into the bottom of the hole.

Especially on a "must make" putt, never look up until the ball is out of your sight. On shorter putts, where it's especially easy to peek too soon, don't look up until you have given the ball plenty of time to reach its destination. This keeps your head from lifting or turning and causing your shoulders to rotate and misdirect the stroke. It also keeps your body from moving and your stroke from decelerating.

I wait one count after impact before allowing myself to look up.

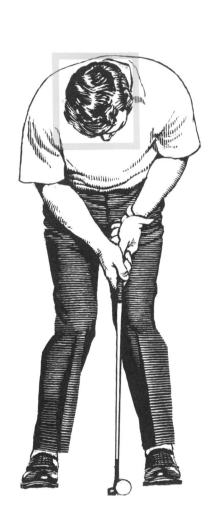

Copy Palmer's quiet head, Archer's bowed legs

Here are two distinctly different putting styles that share an admirable stability. Both methods keep body movement to a minimum. The less body movement in putting, the better. The only exception is on a long putt when you have to move your legs some to keep the stroke flowing through.

Arnold Palmer is famous for his knock-kneed stance. Palmer is so stable because his head stays extremely quiet. It never moves. And if you have trouble moving your lower body on the short and medium putts, bow your legs the way George Archer does. Of course George has a built-in advantage. He used to be a cowboy!

Putting in the wind, crouch and widen your stance

Putting is probably the most difficult thing to do in the wind. The wind is moving you, and it's like trying to shoot at a moving target.

Staying in balance is vital. I widen my stance and crouch a little to anchor myself. When the wind's blowing on the green, I'm glad I'm five nine instead of six two, but sometimes I wish I weighed fifty pounds more. This kind of setup posture can restrict your turn on a full swing, but when you're putting, you want to minimize body motion.

35

MENTAL TIP

This chapter has dealt primarily with the mechanics of the putting stroke, and they are worth all the attention we've paid them. Now I want to caution you about filling your mind with mechanical thoughts when you address a putt in the real world, with a couple of dollars at stake. By then you should have practiced the mechanics until they have become almost second nature. Once you're over the ball, too many thoughts about mechanics can ruin your stroke.

You want a clear mind and a firm, decisive stroking action. All I think about is accelerating the putter through the ball and making solid contact. I want to meet the ball with the sweet spot of the putter.

By thinking about making solid contact, your mind is fixed on a positive thought, which prevents you from thinking negatively.

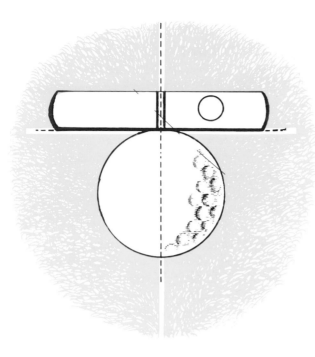

Draw cross hairs to check your aim

A lot of golfers never know whether they're aiming the putter accurately. To get used to setting the putterface squarely behind the ball, put down two cross hairs on the practice green with either string or chalk that won't mar the grass. Be sure the vertical cross hair points at the cup (we're assuming a straight putt). Place a ball at the point where the cross hairs meet, and set the putter in line with the target.

Accelerate on line between 2-by-4s

I think of my stroke as a "popping" stroke. I guide the putter with the left hand on the backswing, change directions with the left still guiding the movement, then accelerate into the ball with the right hand.

Take the putterhead back a certain distance, then swing it a greater distance down the path to the target with an accelerating motion. A very good drill to aid your down-the-line acceleration is practicing with a couple of two-by-fours (or two parallel clubs) set slightly wider apart than the length of your putterhead. Practice short putts and ingrain the feeling of your putter accelerating down the line.

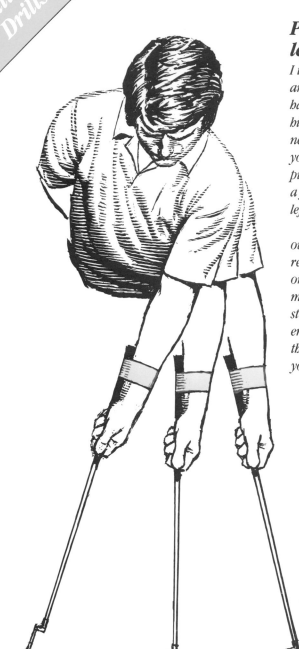

Putt with the left arm only

I take the putter back with the left hand and guide it through the ball with the left hand in my stroke, even though I feel I'm hitting with the right hand. You should never let the left hand and wrist go limp as you hit through the ball. I'll practice short putts using my left arm only, to sharpen a feeling of leading the stroke with the left arm.

I might even slip a tennis sweatband over my wrist and the putter to firm up the relationship between my arm and the club, or I'll lock the putter against the inside of my left forearm (as I'm doing here) and stroke the ball that way. Be sure and accelerate your left arm and the putter through the ball, taking as short a backswing as you can and still make a smooth stroke.

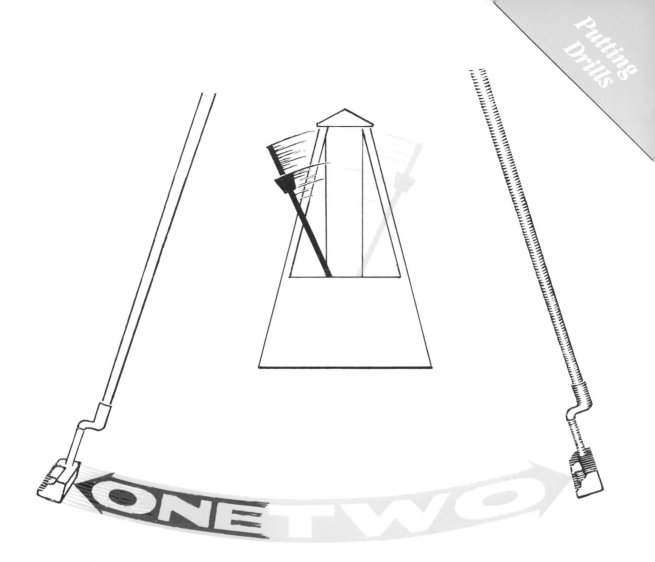

Count to two for smooth pace

I like simple thoughts for tempo, and this one is as elementary as counting "one, two" (with apologies to Lawrence Welk.) I've always said that any dummy who can count to two can make a smooth stroke, and by that I mean "one" on the backswing and "two" on the forward swing.

I'll count to myself that way when I'm practicing, out loud even. Make sure you aren't already to "one and a half" by the time you hit the putt. Think of a metronome with its repeatability and jerk-free change of directions. That's what you want in your putting stroke.

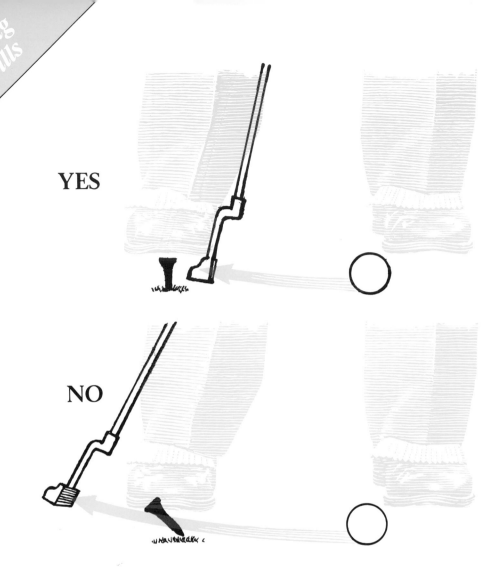

YES

NO

Curtail your takeway with a backstop

Acceleration is all-important in putting, and you can develop it by practicing a shorter backstroke and longer follow-through. Put a tee down opposite your right big toe to help you discipline yourself. Now make a firm, compact stroke—if you hit the tee on your takeaway, your stroke is too long.

Try to hit the ball firmly and determine the distance you can hit it consistently with the shortest stroke. Simple fact: the shorter the stroke, the less chance the putterhead can open or close, causing misdirection of the ball.

Beware of a jerky change of direction from backswing to follow-through. Short is good only as long as it's smooth.

Practice three-footers all around the hole

A good practice routine my father taught me when I started missing short putts is to put twenty balls all around a hole, three feet away, and try to make every one. It's an excellent drill if you pick a hole on a slope, because you'll face every kind of three-footer: uphill, downhill, sidehill left to right, sidehill right to left and all the combinations.

Since you have to change position to hit each putt, you're forced to take your setup seriously on every one. Any poor short putter who practices this routine will get better.

Just roll long putts "inside the leather"

You probably know the expression "inside the leather." You usually hear it in friendly weekend games when putts are conceded if they're inside the grip end of the putter. It's easy to stick the blade in the hole and measure with the putter to tell whether a putt is good.

To make your long putting more consistent and cut down on three-putting, practice rolling the ball inside the leather from 30 to 40 feet. Don't try to sink the putts—just hit to an imaginary circle around the hole and try to leave yourself with second putts no longer than three feet. I credit this drill to Jackie Burke, who used it when he won the 1956 Masters with only one three-putt green.

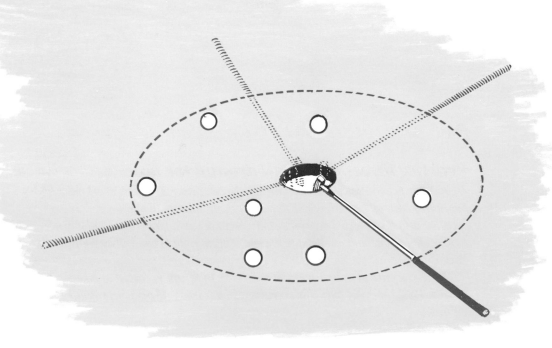

Putt three balls—the last two without looking

Distance is more significant than direction as putts get longer. Aiming comes almost naturally, but judging the speed of a putt demands more practice. People three-putt less because they misread putts than because they misjudge the distance or don't hit the ball solidly.

When I'm putting well, I can place two balls 40 feet from the hole, putt the first ball and then putt the second ball without looking up—and hit the first ball with the second. That's a good drill. Take three balls and putt the last two as if you were blind-folded.

You learn to feel the correct stroke for the distance and make solid contact consistently.

Putt to targets at different distances

Another way to improve your feel for distance is to putt balls at a series of targets spaced about three feet apart. The first target might be 15 feet, the last one 45 (you can poke tees in a practice green to define your distances). Start out working from the short target to the long one, then reverse the operation.

If you want to keep going, putt to different targets at random. Take each putt seriously, though. Go through your regular aiming and setup routine every time. You'll make your routine more consistent at the same time you gain a better feel for distance.

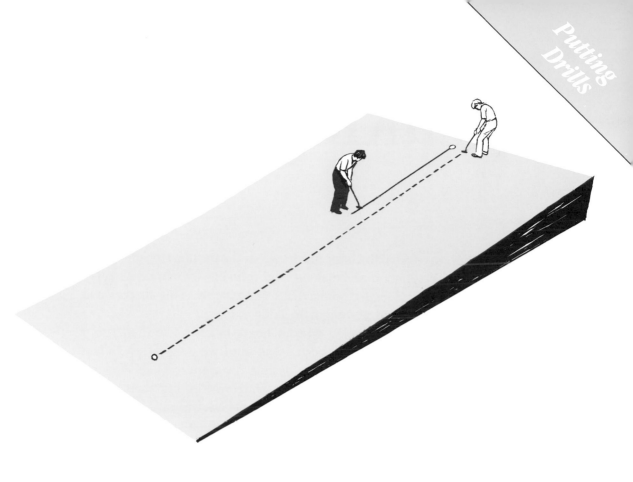

Develop feel by putting uphill, then downhill

Here is the best practice game I know for learning feel, and this business of putting is almost entirely feel. This drill teaches you to judge distance, and is sure to help beginners and advanced players alike.

First, try a 30-foot uphill putt from one hole to another on the practice green, ten times. Memorize the feel and firmness of that uphill stroke. Don't worry where the ball goes—just get a good, solid stroke working. Now try the same putt coming back downhill, stroking ten balls with the identical firmness and solidness you applied going uphill. *See how far the downhill putts scoot past the hole. You've had your first and most important lesson in judging speed.*

Repeat the drill from shorter distances—20 feet, 15 feet, 10 feet, 5 feet. Putt uphill first, then downhill, with the same firmness of stroke. Go through the various putts again, only this time putt downhill first, then uphill. See how far short you leave the uphill putts.

Good golfing instinct can be developed; feel can be taught. This drill proves it.

Breaking Putts

Now that we've covered the basic mechanics of the putting stroke—essentially they are acceleration and making solid contact—let's go on to apply them on real greens designed somewhat to deceive us. This chapter will deal with the reading and playing of breaking putts.

Many of the greens we play on tour break much more than you'd guess watching us on television. I can't wait until we get 3-D TV. Then you'll be able to see what we're up against on a course like Augusta National. All the Masters greens look flat on television, but there isn't a straight putt of any length on the course. People ask how we can miss a six-footer. Well, that six-footer might break a foot and a half!

A friendly word of advice: Read your putts promptly and briskly. Dallying on the greens is a major cause of slow play. Read your putts as soon as you reach the green. Be observant watching others putt—especially if their putts go the same direction as yours. Every bit of information helps.

Study the green
as you approach it

Observing the green as you walk up to it after hitting your approach shot is the first way to size up a putt. Every green has a basic slope, owing to the lay of the land. You can see the predominant slope from 40 yards away better than you can at close range.

The general slope gives you the first (and sometimes most important) impression of the speed of the putt.

Watch your chip shots finish

Keep in mind the impression of the slope you gained from a distance playing a short shot onto the green. Too many golfers play these little shots straight at the flagstick when they'd never treat a long putt so casually. Play the slope on these shots as carefully as you would a putt; sometimes you'll want to go up and quickly survey the green.

After you hit a chip shot onto the green, pay keen attention to how the ball breaks. Watch the entire shot. You will gain a good idea how your putt is going to break.

Read putts with your feet

The putting green is virtually the only place you can survey the entire shot—take advantage of it! Most people rely solely on their eyes to read a putt. It's better to use as many senses as you can, and I learn a lot about a putt by *feeling it with my feet*. I walk from the ball to the cup, close to the line, looking at the line as I walk and feeling with my feet which way the ground slopes.

I also like to check a putt from the usual vantage points: behind the ball, behind the hole and from the side. I try to get as low as I can—I'd lie flat on my stomach if it wasn't so hard on the green and on clothes—and I keep my eyes level. But I derive much of my basic information from walking alongside the line.

Favor the "pro side"

Almost always on Wednesday I will get at least one incredulous expression and a comment from a pro-am partner: "Play that much break? You've got to be kidding!"

Once, on the Broadmoor West Course in Colorado, I played 25 feet of break on a 60-foot putt.

Most weekend golfers share an unhappy tendency to underread putts. They almost never play enough break. I tend to play too much break. My way, a putt at least has a chance to drop in on the high side of the hole as the ball dies. On the low side it has no chance. You hear about missing a putt on the pro side. That simply means you play plenty of break. If you're going to miss, miss on the pro side.

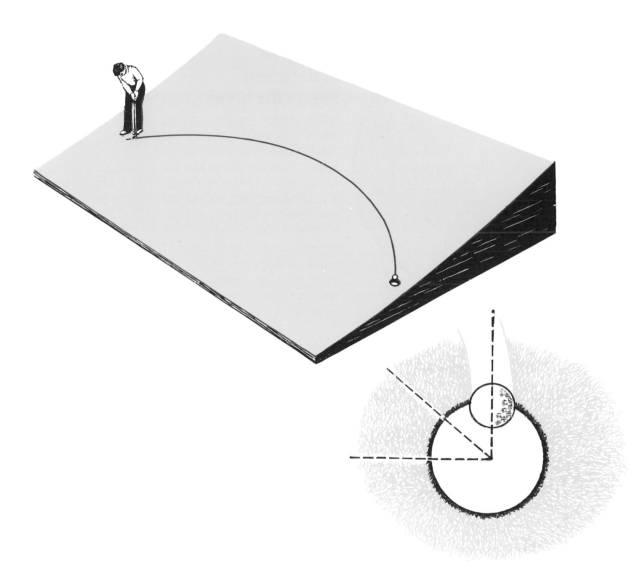

Visualize the center of the cup changing

On all sidehill putts, consider that the center of the hole effectively shifts, and you have to visualize the center differently. You hear television commentators say a pro hit a breaking putt right in the center of the cup, but that's not correct. The "high side" of the cup becomes the center, and that's where you want the ball to enter. I've even had the ball drop in—literally—the back of the hole.

    If the ball has stopped on a side slope and you have to hit it softly, realize that the ball will start to fall off line immediately. On a downhill six-footer with four inches of break, you might have to play a whole foot of break due to the sideslope.

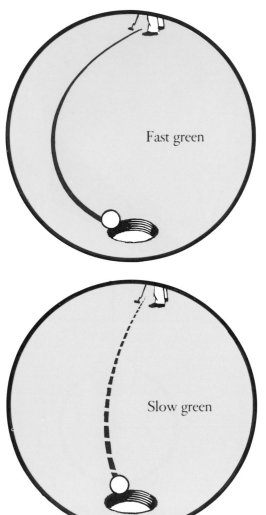

Fast green

Slow green

The speed of the green affects the break

Here's a simple fact about putting that should not be overlooked. The ball will break more on fast greens than on slow greens, because you need less force to get the ball to the hole and the ball encounters less friction.

Play more break on fast greens, because when the ball begins to die it's going to curve more. If you're coming downhill on a fast green, the situation is magnified.

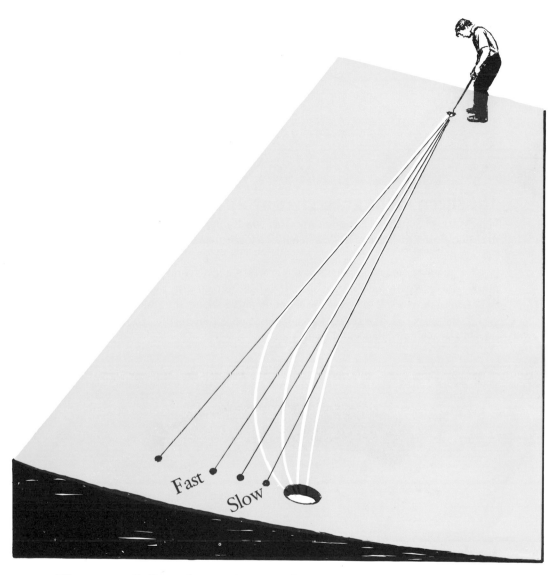

Fast

Slow

How much break to play on faster greens

Here we're looking at the same right-to-left breaking putt—let's call it 25 feet—charted on greens of different speeds. The faster the green, the more break you play. A putt that breaks an inch on a slow green might break 15 inches on a fast green. Because the speed will change from one green to the next, I want to hit the ball a given distance, not a given speed. I want to leave the ball, if I miss, a foot to two feet beyond the hole.

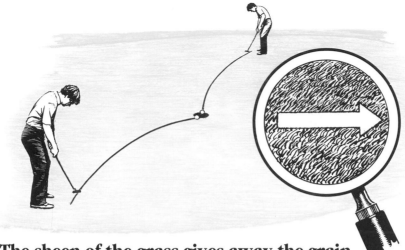

The sheen of the grass gives away the grain

Have you ever putted indoors on a carpet that you assumed was perfectly level—and had the ball consistently break off a straight line? That's the nap of the rug. On the green we call it grain.

The grain of the grass is the direction in which it grows and lays. Especially when putting slow greens, a golfer must play for the grain. You can assay the grain by looking at the sheen of the grass. If the grass is shiny or brighter looking, the grain runs away from you. If the grass is dull or darker looking, the grain is running into you. The ball will travel faster with the grain and sluggishly into it.

Look at the cup to see the grain

Did you ever have a straight, three-foot putt that broke and missed the hole, and you were sure you hit it on line? You missed it due to a cross grain.

In surveying a putt, part of my routine always is to look at the area around the hole for an indication of grain. The grass will grow across the edge of the cup in the direction that it's lying. Grass overhangs the upgrain side of the cup, and dirt shows on the downgrain side. Consider too that the grain is going to influence a ball more when it slows down near the hole.

54

Be aware of mower grain

Have you ever seen a ball snake across a green, wavering both left and right? That's caused by mower grain. Mowing machines create grain in a green, because grass lays in the direction it is cut.

Mowers leave an easily detected light- or dark-green strip when they go back and forth—about three feet wide with the larger, riding mowers and about a foot and a half wide with the smaller, push mowers. These strips indicate the direction of the mower grain.

Mower grain is critical on slow greens where the grass is long, causing the grain to be stronger. You will miss putts if you don't play the mower grain.

For instance, if you face a level 10-foot putt on a slow green and you're heading through three mower stripes, you will have to play the ball to break in the direction of the grain of the two mower stripes that run the same way.

Pick an aiming point

After determining the break of the putt, I pick an aiming point either to the left or to the right of the hole. If the putt breaks a foot from right to left (as in the illustration), I'll aim a foot to the right.

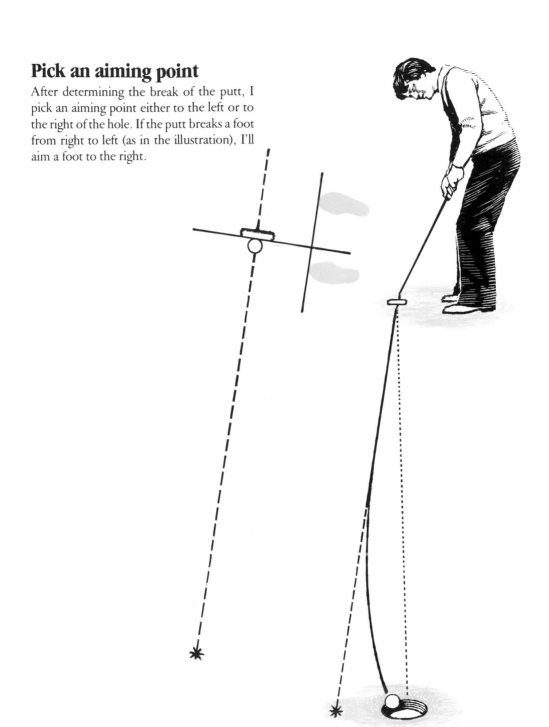

Use your caddie as an aiming aid

Having picked a point at which to aim the putter, I like to have my caddie Bruce Edwards stand "above" the hole, on the high side, so I can aim at him. I might aim at his inside foot, for instance. Then I try to hit the ball straight on that line.

Spot-putt on big breaks

On a lot of greens we play, I sometimes have to allow for much more break than the width of the caddie's feet. On the 16th hole at Pebble Beach the last day of the 1982 Open I had to play 12 feet of break on a 50-foot putt. On a long, severely breaking putt like that one, you should spot-putt. Pick an intermediate spot along the break of the putt—closer to your ball than to the hole—and just roll the ball over that spot. It's the same principle as in spot-bowling. A target close to you is easier to hit than one far away.

Always see some break

I always want to read a break into a putt if it's longer than five or six feet. Most tour pros do. I was playing with a fellow one day who asked his caddie which way a putt broke, and the caddie said, "There's no break, sir—it's straight." That player said he didn't want to hear that, he wanted to know which way it broke!

I want to aim a putt at the left center of the hole or the right center, not dead center. I'll pick a tuft of grass or anything I can find to aim it. There's always something if you look closely. I want some kind of break in the putt so I concentrate more closely and give myself more margin for error.

How to deal with a double break: simple subtraction

One of the toughest putts for all of us is a long, double-breaking putt. The ball curves one
way starting out, then curves back the other way to the hole. The key to the problem is
to determine the difference in the amounts of the two breaks.
Divide the putt into the two slopes. Visualize the first slope and how much the ball
will break. Then visualize the second slope and how much the ball will break back the
other way. Now simply subtract the smaller break from the larger break to determine
your aiming point on the side of the most break.

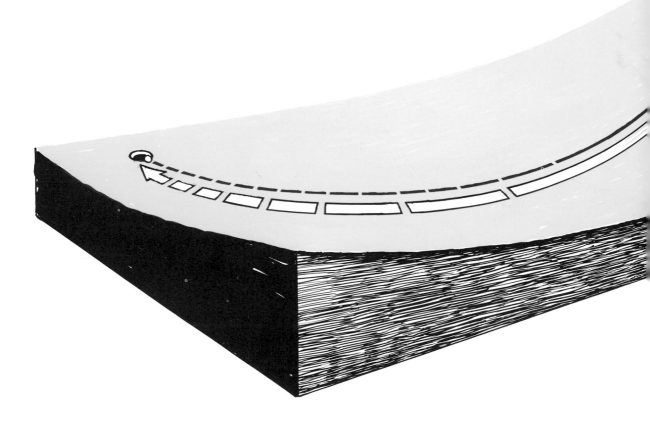

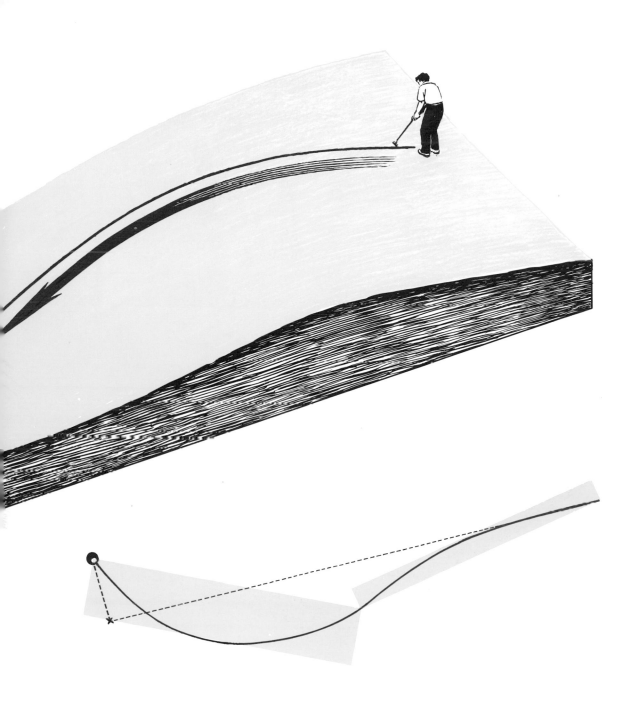

Watch a putt
go past the hole

I'm known as an aggressive putter who seldom leaves the ball short of the hole. I'm not
foolhardy—I will try to die a fast downhill
putt at the hole—but by and large I deserve
my reputation. One advantage of putting
aggressively is that when you knock the ball
past the hole you can see the break you'll
face coming back.

Many amateurs hit a putt too hard and
turn away in disgust because the ball's heading beyond the hole. I watch closely as a
putt goes by the hole, because I get a good
idea how the comeback putt will break.

MENTAL TIP

Obviously, reading and aiming are very important, but you should know from the onset that it's equally important to think you are going to make your putts. If you think you're probably going to miss a putt because you're indecisive about the line or speed or your stroke, you'll miss it for sure.

A lot of putts are missed because of confusion or changing the mind in the middle of the stroke. Choosing an exact line and making a good, solid hit every time is the first step to developing confidence, even if you miss a putt or two along the way. And confidence is a requisite to good putting.

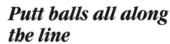

Putt along a string to visualize break

I like this practice drill of Jerry Pate's, in which he lays a string along the path he thinks a curving putt will follow. He putts along the string, then adjusts the string based on what his ball did, then putts again. If you really want to make it fun, put the string down for a 40-foot putt that breaks two different ways and determine your spot-aiming point.

Putt balls all along the line

Having visualized the overall curve of a long practice putt, break it down into three-foot segments and put a ball down every three feet along the line. Now putt every ball and check your impression of the line each time as you work your way back from the hole. You will gain a sense of the overall curve of the putt and the correct aiming point, as well as a closer feel for the distance-direction combination you want on breaking putts.

Chipping and Pitching

Grips and Other Things

Let's move back from the green now to chip and pitch the ball. We saw that putting is a game in itself, and we need to adjust our mechanics and thought processes somewhat for recovery shots around the green, since now we deal not only with the roll of the ball but also with its flight and bounce.

Playing the short shots is really not as difficult as you may think. Your basic guideline, as obvious as it sounds, is to judge the shot properly so you *give yourself the best opportunity to get the ball close.* Too many players don't do that kind of advance planning. They simply choose whatever their favorite club might be, swing and just hope the ball winds up somewhere in the vicinity of the cup.

The one critical factor in the short game is *distance feel:* knowing how far the ball will carry and then roll. Given the same swing, the distance the ball will go varies with the loft of the club you have in your hands, the texture, moisture content and contouring of the green, and the wind. Learning how far the ball will go with all of these variables affecting the outcome is the art, or secret, of golf itself. I will be discussing all of these variables, but first some general rules for chips and pitches:

• Club selection is crucial in the short game. A skilled player, such as the great Bobby Locke, may be able to make one club—a pitching wedge or sand wedge, say—work for all chips and pitches, but I think the majority of golfers should use different clubs for different situations and lies (more about lies later). Simply let the club's normal loft do the work rather than use a different and sometimes more difficult swing technique.

- Always spot-chip and spot-pitch, which simply means aiming at a point on the green where you want the ball to land and letting it run from there to the target. This is the way I practiced as a youngster, and I find it the best way to develop distance feel and consistency.

- Always try to land the ball on the green. This prevents bad bounces on the longer, uneven fringe and rough turf around the green.

- Try not to land the ball on any severe slope—uphill, downhill or sidehill. It's harder to judge the angle of the bounce from these slopes. Land the ball on flat areas of the green whenever possible. At the Tournament Players Championship I've played a sand wedge to loft chip shots over severe contours and land the ball on the flatter area around the cup.

Now let's prepare to play the shots.

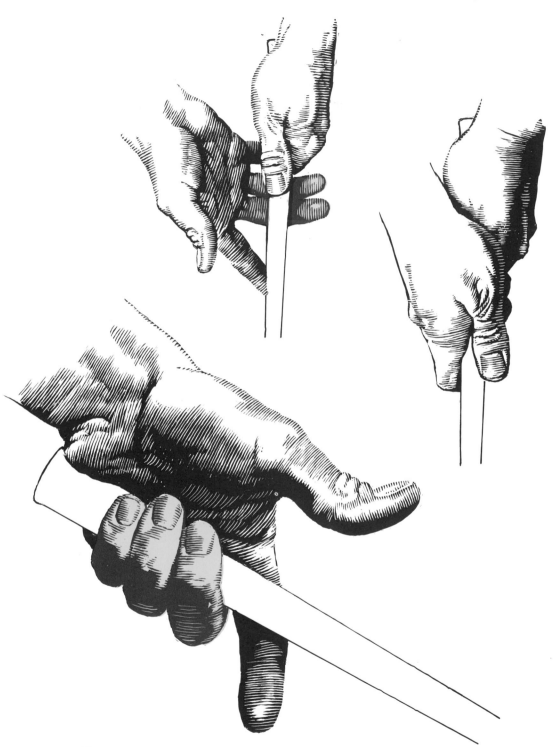

How to hold the club

It is virtually impossible to play your best golf without a good grip to keep the club from slipping in your hand. Without a good grip, you can never reach your full potential as a golfer.

Occasionally I will use the reverse overlapping grip, or my putting grip, for a short chip shot. But for most of my chip shots and all my pitch shots I use the basic Vardon overlapping grip, sometimes weakening my grip to hit high shots or sand shots. The club in my Vardon grip rests diagonally across my left hand, running from the first joint of the forefinger to just under the pad. The left thumb isn't straight down the shaft—it's just off center to the right. In the right hand, the club lays in the fingers, not in the palm—across the ring finger and middle finger and cleanly against the index finger, with a slight gap between the middle finger and index finger. This allows the forefinger and thumb, which rests down the left center of the shaft, to "cradle" the club for greater feel and control. The little finger of my right hand overlaps the left hand in the indentation between the index and middle fingers, and the lifeline of my right hand overlaps the thumb of my left hand.

I apply most of the pressure in holding the club with the last three fingers of the left hand. The left thumb and forefinger apply very little pressure at all. In the right hand, the ring and middle fingers are the anchor points.

I apply as much pressure in the last three fingers of my left hand as possible without creating tension in my forearms. My left forearm is firm but not rigid. The right-hand pressure is less than in my left hand, with very little at all in the right thumb and forefinger. The common fault is to hold the club too tightly in both hands because of a bad grip, which makes the arms too rigid.

Experiment on the practice tee to find the right grip pressure for you. Start with the lightest possible grip pressure in your hands and gradually increase it until you find the amount of pressure that lets you control the club—not letting it slip at all in your hands.

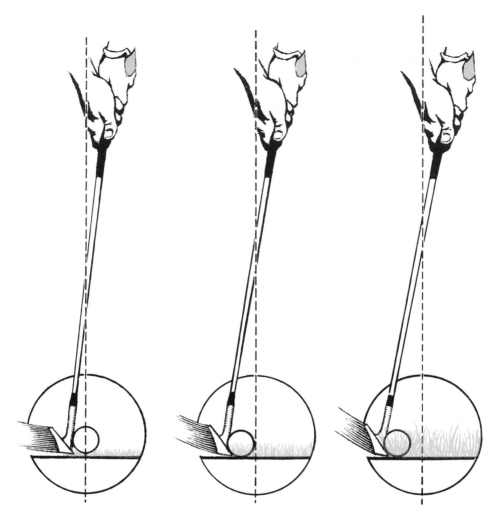

Check the lie first

The lie of the ball tells you what club to choose. The lie is a primary influence on shotmaking, and one that many golfers underestimate. The worse the lie, the more I'll tend to play the ball back in my stance. Playing the ball back and keeping my hands ahead of the ball through impact will produce a more descending blow and solid contact.

Generally I'll use a less lofted club (a 7-, 8- or 9-iron) from an uphill lie, because of the built-in loft the lie provides. Conversely, I'll use a more lofted club (pitching or sand wedge) for a downhill lie, which takes loft off.

If the ball is in long grass that lies in the opposite direction of the shot I'm going to play, I'll consciously try to hit the ball harder. Conversely, if the ball is lying downgrain, I'll hit it easier.

So always examine closely the lie of the ball to determine what the ball is likely to do. This makes it much easier to choose the right club for the best results.

See the shot before you play it

The most important aspect of any shot is to visualize what you want to do before you address the ball and swing. Visualization is creating a game plan. Visualize the ball flying through the air, bouncing, then rolling up to the hole.

One of my best examples of visualizing a shot occurred in the 1981 U.S. Open at Merion. The ninth hole is a par 3 with a deep bunker to the right front of the green. After a pushed 6-iron shot, my ball ended up in the right portion of the bunker on a downhill lie. The lip of the bunker was at least shoulder high, and there was a treacherous downslope falling away from the top of the bunker to the pin, which was cut close to my side of the green. I visualized a six-inch landing area just over the lip, and then popped the ball up and hit that spot. The ball rolled down about three feet short of the hole.

Not every shot turns out like that one, obviously. There are days when I have poor feel and play badly, but even on those days I visualize or plan every shot I play.

Develop a consistent pre-shot routine

Before we move on to the basics of the chipping stroke, it's worth pointing out that after visualizing the shot and taking their practice swings, good players have a precise pre-shot routine which repeats itself consistently. My pre-shot routine consists of (in order) aiming the clubface on the intended line of flight, taking my stance, looking at the target and then back at the ball, waggling the clubhead while looking at the target one last time, one last waggle, then starting the swing.

The pre-shot routine is actually the beginning of a series of movements leading into the stroke itself. An individual pre-shot routine varies from one golfer to the next—the number of practice swings, waggles, glances from the ball to the target—but most good golfers use precisely the same routine for every shot they play.

Bert Yancey once made a study of the pros on the PGA Tour, measuring the time we took from the time we addressed the ball to the time we hit it. He found that the pre-shot routine of nearly every pro varied by less than one second. Develop a consistent pre-shot routine and your play will become more consistent too.

The Basic Chipping Stroke

Chipping is your most important asset for scoring better. Improve your chipping and you automatically improve your scoring. Learn to feel the right distance and choose the correct club consistently, and you can easily save five strokes a round. Yet chipping is probably the least-practiced part of the game and the most neglected.

Chipping is feel and simple mechanics. I will deal with both in the form of illustrations, text descriptions and simple practice drills that will help you learn to feel the distance by instinct as I do.

I'll stress simple concepts that anyone can learn. For instance, with rare exceptions I do not try to put spin on the ball. I don't try to hit sharply down on it or impart sidespin. I try to meet the ball with a square clubface and make solid contact every time so I can get consistent distance out of each club. I want to let the face of the club do its job. You can close the face to make the ball run more, or open the face to make it pop up (a particularly risky option, since you have less clubface to work with), but basically that's not the way I play or recommend you play. Spin is not part of my chipping approach. I want the ball to land and behave as predictably as possible. The less spin on the ball, the more consistency you gain.

Club selection is as important as execution. I almost always would rather putt than chip from off the green if the fringe grass is well manicured and firm, the way it is at Augusta National, for instance. I figure that my worst putt will almost always be better than my worst chip. Play your best odds on a shot.

Otherwise I will use any club from a wedge to a 5-iron depending on the circumstances. I've never been an advocate of one-club chipping except as a practice device. You face too many different shots to restrict yourself to one club. Varying your club selection adds more shots to your range of possibilities. (I just wish clubs originally had been numbered in reverse order, with the 1-iron being the shortest and the 9-iron the longest. Then you could talk about using more club or less club and everyone would know what you mean.)

When I was a youngster I played a wedge most of the time around the green, like the great Bobby Locke, who was an excellent chipper. I'd try to hit a high-lofted shot up to the hole no matter where I was. I got away with it much of the time because I was young and had the nerves of a neurosurgeon. But I finally learned after too many "three to get down" holes to use different clubs to fit different shots. I learned there's one ideal way to play every shot with the best odds of success. You have to educate yourself to find it by practicing the entire process of shot visualization, club selection and swing execution.

That's what this chapter and the next one will help you do. Let's start chipping away at your handicap.

The chipping stroke
In this basic chipping sequence you will notice the address position with the hands ahead of the ball and the stance slightly open. The stroke is dominated by the left arm, with lower-body movement making it possible to keep the wrists firm through impact.

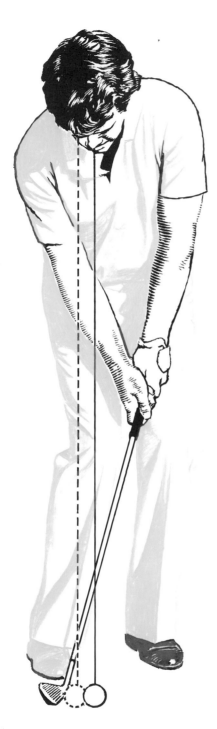

Set your hands ahead of the clubhead

The most fundamental mechanic of chipping is to address the ball with most of your weight on your left foot and your hands ahead of the clubhead, or toward the hole. By doing this, you are assured of accelerating the club into the ball with a descending blow.

I want my hands ahead of the ball and the ball no farther forward than the middle of my stance, or about in line with my nose, so the hands can lead the clubhead into the ball. I want to hit the ball before I hit the ground. The poorer the lie, the farther back I position the ball, to strike a *more* descending blow.

My feet and body are aligned 10 to 20 degrees open to the target, putting me into position to swing the club straight out toward the hole with firm wrist action.

Hale Irwin told President Ford to put his hands ahead of the clubhead at address, and the President's chipping improved dramatically.

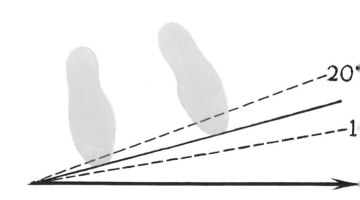

Choke down consistently
with your chipping clubs

Grip down on your chipping clubs for control—halfway to the steel at least. But grip down to the exact same point on every club, to standardize the feel from one club to the next. I hear weekend golfers say that different clubs have different feels. That's because they grip one club short and another one long. So grip down to the identical spot on every club.

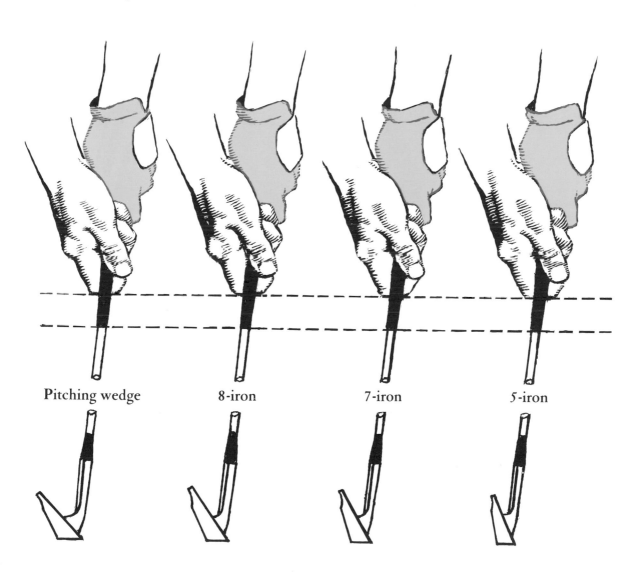

Pitching wedge   8-iron   7-iron   5-iron

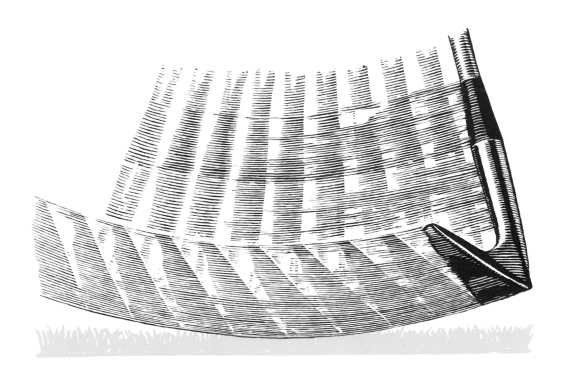

Just brush the grass

Once you're set up to the ball correctly, the chipping stroke is merely brushing the grass with the club. Sole the club very lightly (the full weight shouldn't even rest on the ground) and make little swings back and forth without a ball to familiarize yourself with the feeling. When the ball's there, just meet it solidly and sweep it away.

Let the right knee go to the target

A technique I use to make chip shots easier is starting the forward swing with my right knee. Swing your arms back, then just move the right knee to the target, rolling to the inside of your right foot. There isn't much leg action in a chip shot—it's almost all arm swing—but *you have to have some body flow*…some freedom in your lower body.

That little movement of the right knee keys the forward swing—it keeps the left arm leading the forward swing, making the hands stay ahead of the clubhead through impact. You won't have the tendency to hit too soon with the right hand and scoop at the ball, causing a fat or skulled shot. Start the forward swing with the right knee moving toward the target, and swing your arms through the ball. You'll get a good, positive acceleration of the clubhead.

Beware of the grain

The grain of the greens (the direction in which the grass grows) will affect your chipping, the same as it does your putting. If the grain's against you, you'll have to swing harder. If it's with you, you'll have to swing easier. The first bounce on the green is the most important, and it pays to check the grain in that area. If the ball lands in a really grainy part of the green, you could end up 10 feet short or long on a 30-foot chip.

Remember that the sheen of the grass shows you the grain. If the grass is shiny, the grain is with me and the ball will roll a greater distance. If the grass is darker or dull looking, the grain's into me and the ball won't roll as far. Chipping to a dark-colored upslope on a slow green, you have to give the shot something extra. Conversely, if you're chipping downhill and the slope is light-complected and fast, you'd better swing easier. The illustration here shows the influence of grain on a flat surface. Particularly notice how the ball bounces.

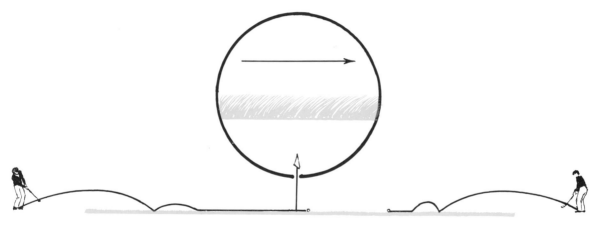

Leave the pin in to chip

I like to leave the flagstick in when I'm chipping. Most importantly, it gives me a backstop, especially on downhill chips that might roll well beyond the cup if the pin was taken out. Another reason is it helps my depth perception when I'm sizing up the shot and figuring the distance. And on longer chips, leaving the flagstick in eliminates any doubts about seeing the hole clearly.

Don't be gone with the wind

A strong wind affects chip shots more than most people realize. On downwind and upwind chips the effect is obvious. If you loft the ball in the air any distance at all in a strong crosswind, the wind's going to work on it. Then when the ball lands, it doesn't land going straight, it lands at an angle and moves sideways some more. Growing up in Kansas, I learned that a 25-mile-an-hour, right-to-left crosswind could cause me to miss the hole three or four feet to the left. That can be the difference between a par and a bogey.

MENTAL TIP

When I visualize a chip shot, I think of it as a chip and a putt combined. It's one shot in the air and another on the ground. I want to see in my mind the spot where I want the ball to land, then envision the ball rolling the rest of the way like a putt.

Chip with your left hand only

The basic chip shot is mainly an arm swing, with very little wrist action. The left arm controls the club, both on the backswing and the follow-through. Practice by swinging the club with the left hand only. Remember to let the right knee move toward the target on the forward swing, which makes the left arm always lead firmly through the hitting area.

Spot-chip to develop feel

This is the first in a series of drills you should practice to become a good chipper. My first thought after I consider the lie of the ball is where I want to land the ball on the green. Simply mark a spot on the green and chip to it with one club until you can land the ball consistently on or very near the spot.

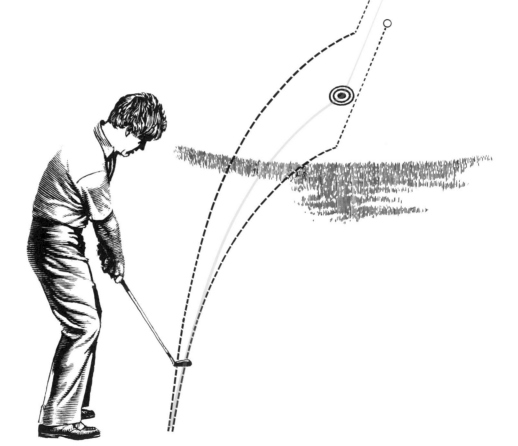

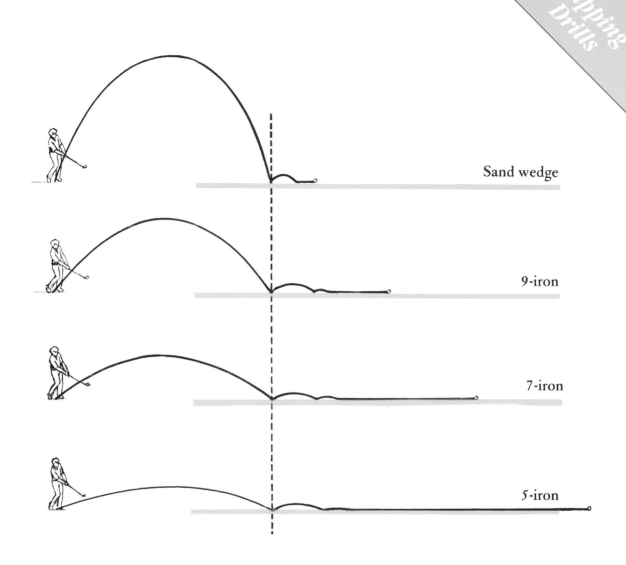

Sand wedge

9-iron

7-iron

5-iron

Chip to the same spot with different clubs

After you've learned to hit one club to a landing spot, take that drill a step further and chip to that same spot with various clubs. Try using a sand wedge, 9-iron, 7-iron, 5-iron. The object of this drill is to carry the ball the same distance in the air with different clubs and observe the different distances the ball will roll.

This is the most important drill you can practice because it teaches you not only how far to hit the ball in the air but also how far the ball rolls on the green.

Deciding which club to use

One you've mastered the previous drill, this simple practice game will teach you to pick the right club for a given shot, taking into account both the carry and roll factors. Simply use different clubs for the same shot. *You will learn to eliminate the clubs that make it difficult to get the ball close, and pick the one that gives you the best, most consistent results.*

Chip to the inner circle

My favorite chipping drill, which I've used since I was a kid, is to chip from different spots around the green to a circle with a three-foot radius. I feel that if I can chip the ball within three feet of the cup, it's a successful shot.

If the chip shot has a lot of break in it, I picture a six-foot corridor leading to the circle. This is the drill I practice the most because it's exactly what I try to do on the golf course.

Chip to the practice green

Here's a good exercise in club selection. Working from one spot off the practice green (assuming your course allows chipping to the practice green), play balls to the different holes using whichever club you think you need. For a short shot to a tight pin position, you might choose a wedge. For a shot that must traverse 60 feet of green, you might take a 6-iron.

When you've hit from one spot to the different holes, go to a new spot and repeat the routine. It's an excellent way to get a good feel for the speed and firmness of the greens before a round and just to develop touch in general.

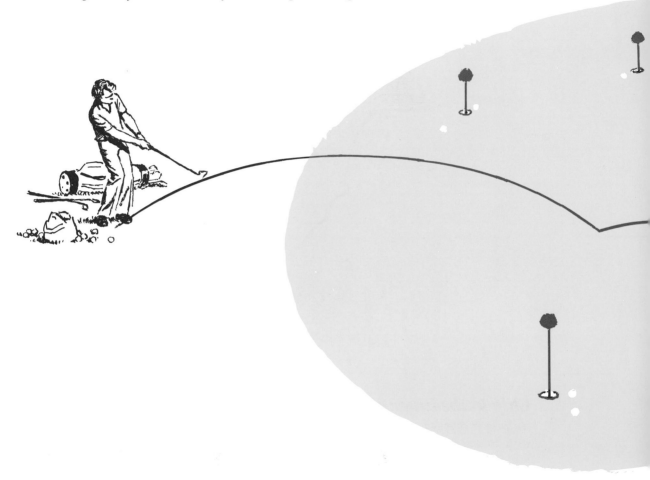

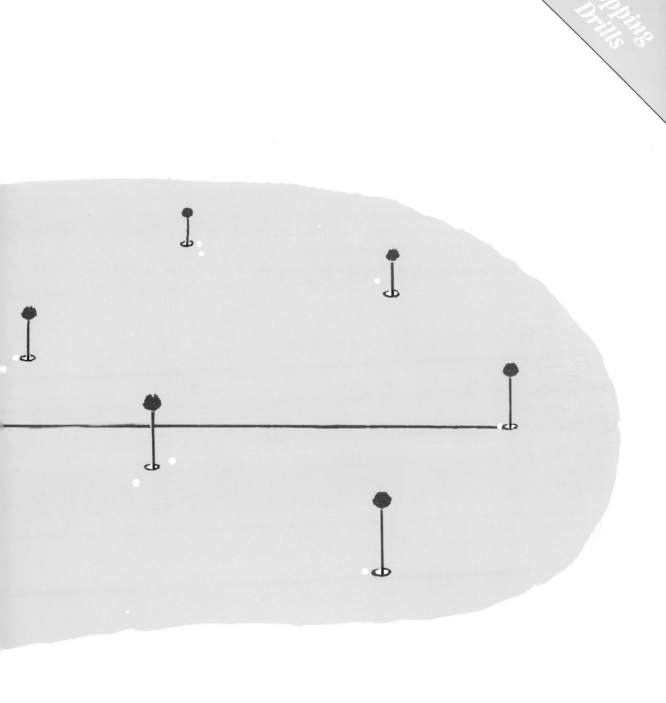

Special Chips

Once you have mastered the basic chipping stroke, you must learn to adjust to the almost endless variety of chip shots you'll encounter on the course. If your fundamentals are sound, you have the base to play different kinds of shots and lop several strokes off your best scores.

Now let's look at some of the more common specialty chips you're apt to face.

Use a putter instead of chipping whenever possible

When you're not on the green and you face a shot where the turf is firm, dry, and cut low, use a putter. More times than not I'll putt from well off the fringe and eliminate chipping entirely. Essentially I believe that my worst putt is always better than my worst chip. At Augusta National the fringes are so wide and well-manicured that I sometimes will putt from several yards off the green.

The ball falls with the slope from sidehill lies

An overlooked factor in golf is that sidehill lies affect short shots just as they do long ones. The rule of thumb is that the ball will fall in the direction of the slope. You must take measures that allow for this and even counteract it to some extent.

When the ball is below your feet, your more upright swing will cause sidespin, which makes the ball fly and run from left to right. Stand slightly closer to the ball, with your weight centered more on your left side and toward your heels just enough so you feel solidly balanced. Bend more at the waist and aim slightly left of your target. When the ball is severely below your feet, you must lengthen the club by gripping more toward its end. Using the full length of the club should make you chip the ball farther because of the increased length of your arc, so you should hit this particular chip easier.

With the ball above your feet, the shot will tend to be pulled left of the target because of the flatter arc of this swing.

Stand a little farther from the ball and play it toward the middle or back of your stance. Again set your weight to the left, but this time more on your toes so you'll maintain good balance. Grip down on the club, aim to the right and swing with the slope. Swing harder on this shot to compensate for the shorter arc that results from gripping down on the club.

From an extreme sidehill lie with the ball above your feet, you must aim *well right* of the target. Especially if you are using a high-lofted club (i.e., sand wedge, pitching wedge, or 9-iron), the flat arc of your swing will pull the ball well left, so *make sure* to aim well right.

Change your setup and club selection for uphill and downhill lies

When you have a short shot from an uphill or downhill lie, you must alter your body position and club selection.

From an uphill lie, the loft of the slope adds to the loft of the club. This makes you hit the ball too high, and makes the distance factor difficult to judge. Choose a less lofted club such as an 8-iron, which gives you a better chance of getting the ball close to the pin, especially if you mis-hit it. Uphill, align your shoulders and body with the slope, with your weight toward your right side, and play the ball more toward your left foot. This allows you to swing along the slope of the hill, rather than digging into it.

Downhill, the loft of the slope subtracts from the loft of the club, and makes the ball fly lower. Choose a pitching wedge or sand wedge, play the ball back, just inside your right foot, and set your weight more on your left side and leave it there during the swing. Aligning your shoulders and body with the slope as much as possible allows you once again to swing with the slope. Remember, the ball will roll farther on the green from a downhill lie, so take that into account.

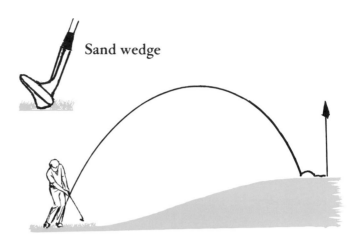

Sand wedge

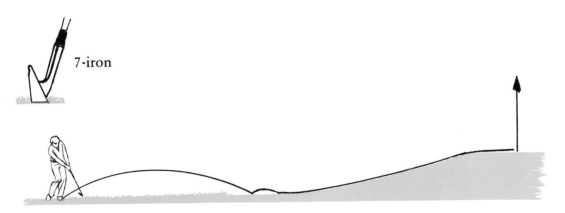

7-iron

The short and long of uphill chips

On a short uphill chip with the flagstick close to me, when I want the ball to land on the green and stop quickly, I use a sand wedge, a pitching wedge or 9-iron. I follow the same procedure I did on the previous page for an uphill shot.

On a long uphill chip I usually take an 8-iron or 7-iron and position the ball more in the middle of my stance. Then I pick a landing spot not far onto the green and let the ball roll the rest of the way from there.

The short and long of downhill chips

On a short downhill chip, like the one I holed on the Pebble Beach 17th in the last round of the 1982 U.S. Open, I use a sand wedge or pitching wedge almost exclusively. I'll open both the clubface and my stance slightly more than for a normal flat lie, still keeping my hands ahead of the ball at address. Through the ball I want to keep the clubface open and lead the clubhead down the slope with my hands.

On a long downhill chip, you have the advantage of being able to land the ball on the green and let it roll like a putt. I'll usually use a 9-iron or sometimes an 8-iron. I use my regular stance—the ball back a little of center—and a square clubface.

A reminder: On all these little touch shots I want to make solid contact and accelerate the clubhead through the ball. You can't baby them.

Chipping out of the rough

I tend to use either a sand or pitching wedge and play chip shots out of the rough in much the same way I play sand shots, as you'll see when we come to the chapters on sand play. With the ball back at least in the middle of my stance, I open both my setup and the clubface. I take the club up more abruptly on the backswing by hinging my right hand sooner, to avoid as much grass as possible on the takeaway. On the forward swing I slide the clubhead under the ball with the face held firmly open by the last three fingers of my left hand. I can even hit slightly behind the ball, as if I were in the sand, with good results. Remember that the ball will tend to run farther from out of the rough than from a regular lie.

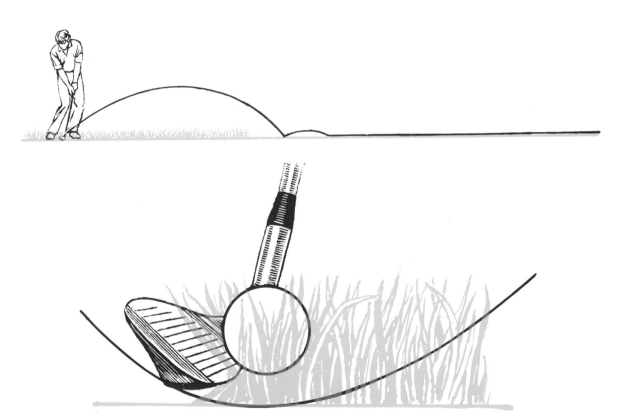

The bump and run over a mound

On a short shot to the green with a mound in the way and the flagstick tucked close to the near edge, it's almost impossible to get a lofted shot anywhere near the hole. Do not use a sand wedge or pitching wedge. Instead, take a less lofted club, a 5-, 6-, or 7-iron, and chip the ball into the upslope so it will bounce up to the top of the mound and then *roll* down the other side onto the green.

The important thing is to have the ball rolling, not bouncing, down the slope.

This is a shot you play frequently on British courses like St. Andrews, and I always practice it before I go over to play in the British Open.

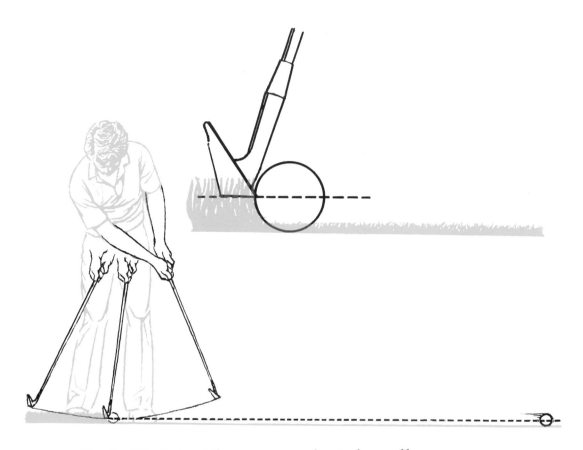

The bellied shot from up against the collar

If the ball's resting right up against the fringe, I use a shot called the "bellied wedge" instead of trying a normal chip shot. I do three things: I use a straight-edged wedge or 9-iron (not a rounded-edged club like a sand wedge); I use my normal putting grip and stroke, and most important, I make contact in the *middle* of the ball. This shot was popularized by Dave Hill and Lee Trevino, and most pros on the tour use it today.

Hit this shot with the same force you would impart to a putt of the same distance, since the ball will roll exactly like a putt.

Handling the chip off hardpan

The vital factor on shots from bare lies is to position the ball in your stance so that you can consistently contact the ball first. Position the ball in the center or just back of center, ensuring that you always hit the ball with at least a slightly downward blow. Make sure your hands are positioned ahead of the clubhead, and just swing normally. I will never use a sand wedge for this shot because the flange will bounce off the hard ground and result in a skulled shot.

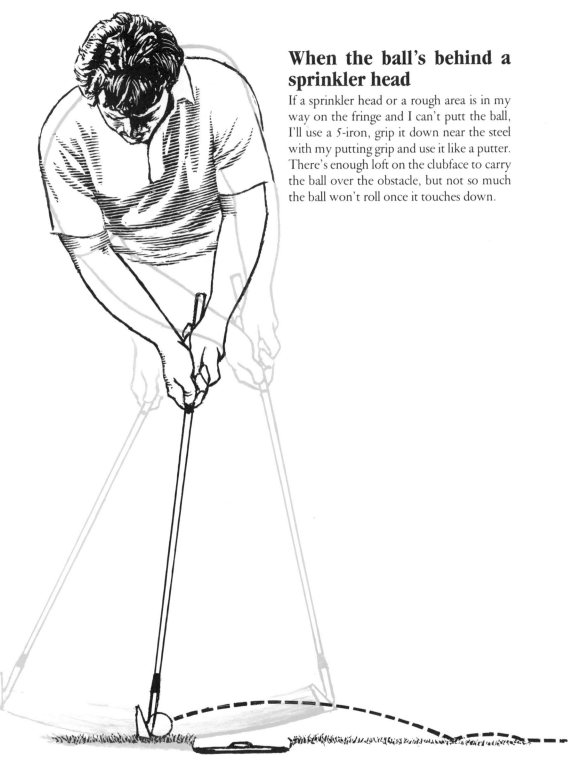

When the ball's behind a sprinkler head

If a sprinkler head or a rough area is in my way on the fringe and I can't putt the ball, I'll use a 5-iron, grip it down near the steel with my putting grip and use it like a putter. There's enough loft on the clubface to carry the ball over the obstacle, but not so much the ball won't roll once it touches down.

The escape from a tree

This is a chip shot you might invoke long before you reach the green area. If your ball ends up on the wrong side of a tree and you're understandably reluctant to hit a left-handed shot, backhand it with your right hand (assuming you're right-handed). Take a wedge if you need to get the ball airborne. With your back to the target, make sure the clubface is square to your intended line, then just lift the club with your right hand and whack down on the back side of the ball. It's strictly an arm motion with not much wrist action.

Be sure to make a few practice swings to see where the club will hit the ground. That's a good idea on any unusual shot.

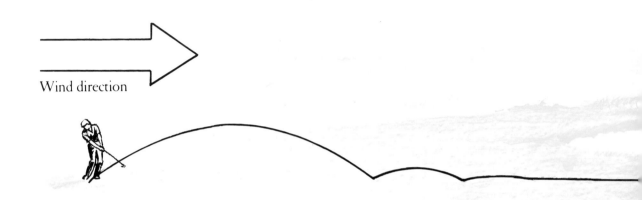

Wind direction

The extra-long chip shot

I've seen a 55-yard chip shot—Ben Crenshaw hit it one day in the Byron Nelson tournament at Preston Trail in Dallas, and it was one of the best chips I've ever seen. We were playing with a hard wind behind us, the fairway was very firm and the green was open in front, a shot one often faces in the British Open. Ben, who has a magnificent short game, chipped the ball with a 5-iron and it carried about ten yards in the air and then just rolled and rolled until it stopped three feet from the hole. If he had lofted the ball with a wedge in this strong tailwind, there's no telling where the ball would have stopped!

The Basic Pitching Stroke

In my opinion, learning how to pitch the ball is the most difficult lesson for a golfer. Why? Because you must learn how to hit the ball with an abbreviated or less-than-full swing. You must feel how far to hit the ball, and feel is the most elusive part of golf.

Almost all golfers practice nothing but a full swing. Very few practice the short, 40-yard pitch shot. A full swing is easier to master, since the golfer is usually repeating the same swing for each club to make the ball go the maximum distance with that particular club. But to hit the ball less than maximum distance with a particular club, you must shorten the swing *yet still hit the ball firmly.* This shot causes many golfers to shake with fear and has resulted in the club as well as the ball being launched in disgust.

The two main requisites to good pitching are setting up well and making a firm swing that accelerates the clubhead through the ball. When you face a less-than-full shot, you have to think in terms of a less-than-full backswing. The common error is taking the club back too far and decelerating through impact, which is like a boxer pulling his punches. It causes all sorts of mis-hit and misdirected pitch shots.

As it was with chipping, my philosophy is to play pitches with as little spin as possible, because spin is hard to control and predict. Learning to pitch the ball with control and finesse, over hazards and near the pin, is a joyful part of the game and an art form in itself.

The pitching stroke

In this chapter on pitching, we'll discuss the value of: the proper setup, including aligning your hands ahead of the ball, and a firm arm swing coordinated with the movement of the lower body.

The proper address position previews the impact position

My setup position here, as in all my shots, is very similar to my impact position—a sneak preview. It's basically the same as my chipping setup. My stance is slightly open, 10 to 20 degrees, since I want my left side to be out of the way or slightly open at impact. The body weight favors the left foot and is centered on the balls of the feet. My knees are slightly flexed, my rear end stuck out so that I can hang my upper body and arms out over the ball. I call my rear end my "ballast." When stuck out properly, it serves as a counterweight to my upper body, which must hang out over the ball so that the arms can swing freely without running into the body on the downswing. I sole the club very lightly.

Two common faulty setup positions are:

1. Standing too tall, which means the upper body doesn't hang over enough. The upper body then must either dip on the backswing or turn too horizontally, forcing the arms and club to swing too flatly around the body. Both of these swings result in poor balance and poor timing, causing inconsistency.

2. The knees are too straight and the body slumps over the ball, forcing too much weight onto the toes. In this position you must rely on perfect hand-eye coordination for consistent shotmaking. With straight, unflexed knees you cannot transfer the weight properly during the swing.

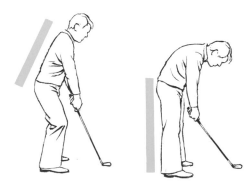

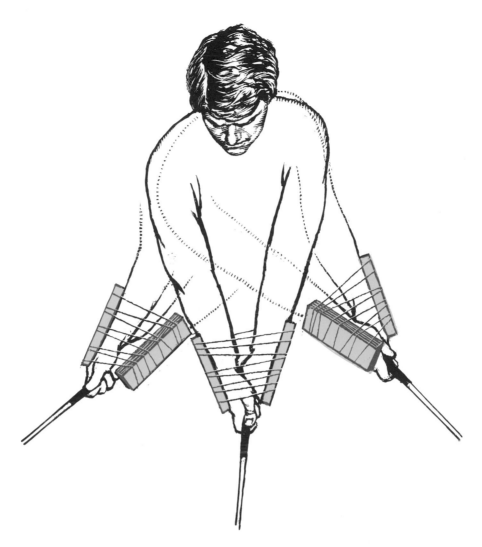

Firm up your wrist action by "wearing splints"

The greatest pitchers in the game are people such as Tom Weiskopf who use very little hand and wrist action. I try to keep from overusing my hands throughout my swing by picturing my wrists held firm by a pair of splints.I feel as if I initiate the takeaway with my hands and arms tied together as a unit. (Don't start the backswing with your hands— your hands and arms must move together.) Only when my right elbow starts to bend will my wrists start to hinge.

Be careful not to "freeze" your wrists by gripping the club too tightly. A tense grip causes you to lose feel. Your grip pressure should be only firm enough to prevent the club from slipping in your hands.

As we will discuss next, you need a good weight transfer to keep your wrists firm. Poor body movement will cause an overuse of the hands.

I advocate Byron Nelson's "rocking chair" weight transfer

The pitch shot is made easier and more consistent when the lower body moves in timing with the arms and hands. Lack of movement in the lower body causes an inconsistent path of the club through impact. I jokingly refer to this bad habit as having "cement legs."

Do not stand still and use just your hands and arms. Use your hips and knees in the swing.

How? I picture Byron Nelson, whose short, firm pitching swing was a smooth blend of both upper and lower body movement. Byron teaches a rocking-chair motion that coordinates the upper and lower body action, making possible a consistent hit time after time.

The weight, which starts mostly on the left foot, transfers to the right foot and back to the left foot during the swing. The hit of the ball occurs during the transfer of weight from the right foot to the left foot. Byron couldn't help but hit the ball solidly and straight. His clubface stayed square just prior to and through impact the longest of any player I've ever watched—for nearly a foot; not only pitching but on his full swing as well.

A simple thought that Byron taught me is to return my hips and elbows to their original address position as I'm hitting through the ball. This forces me to synchronize the motion of my arms and lower body.

Accelerate the clubhead and don't overswing

Tom Kite, who is an excellent pitcher from 30 and 40 yards with a wedge, makes sure to avoid the common pitfall of decelerating the club through the impact zone. Tom's key thought is to swing the club back only as far as he swings it through.

Many high-handicap players swing with little or no weight transfer. Therefore they have to take the club back too far in the effort to produce the same clubhead speed they could produce with a proper weight transfer and a shorter swing. If you have a problem overswinging, first check your weight transfer. Then try swinging the club back shorter and accelerating it more firmly through the ball.

Make an underhanded motion

Golf is an underhanded game. Since we're swinging down at the ball, we have to use an underhanded motion with the right hand and arm through the impact area. You can get the feeling by throwing a ball, because the underhanded motion we're talking about is similar to a throwing action.

The return of the right elbow

Many good teachers and players have advocated this point, and I agree with them: the key to making a good underhanded motion is to keep the right elbow close to your body during the downswing. It can swing free on your backswing, as the result of your shoulders turning and your arms and hands swinging the club up, but it *must* return close to your body on the downswing.

Some good players even like to brush the right elbow across the right hip coming into the ball. If the right elbow returns close to your side, the straightening out (or release) of the entire right side will be consistent and well timed.

MENTAL TIP

Once you've begun to master the fundamentals of the basic pitch-shot stroke, visualizing a shot before you hit becomes all-important. I've said it before about shorter shots, and I want to say it again here about pitching, because for some reason most golfers forget it as they get farther from the hole.

You have to visualize first of all the spot where you want the ball to land. Preferably you want to land the ball on the green and on a flat part of the green. On a shot of 30 or 40 yards it can be worthwhile to walk up quickly and survey your landing area before you play the shot.

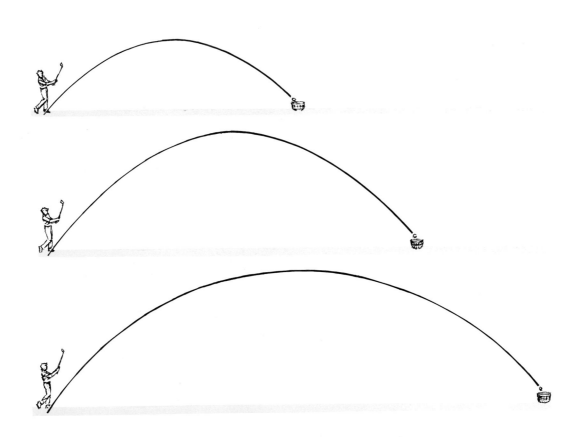

Pitch to different targets

Set targets out at, say, 15, 25 and 40 yards and pitch to them alternately. Start with the shortest shot and work up to the longest, then mix up your shots.

I also like to practice varying the trajectory of the ball with a particular club. I might take a sand wedge and see how low and high I can hit it to the various targets.

Practice from poor lies too

Does your ball always end up in a good lie? Obviously not. Practice from bad lies to learn how the ball flies out of poor lies—from the rough, for example—so that when you're on the golf course you'll be prepared for a variety of situations. A lot of golfers might practice from a bad lie once, but they won't practice from that lie ten times, which is what you have to do to become a complete player.

Play different shots with the same club

This is the tough one, for advanced players. I like to drop my practice balls all the way around an interesting green and play a variety of chips and pitches with one club, a 7-iron perhaps. This teaches you to use your imagination and improvise shots.

If you have to hit a 7-iron over a bunker to a tight pin position, you lay the blade wide open, aim well left, take the club back outside the target line and slide the club-head under the ball. Most people have no idea how to play a shot like that, but they can figure it out if they have to. To concoct shots like that, you have to picture them in your mind before you hit them. This drill develops your ability to visualize. You have to be able to see a trouble shot in advance to be able to play it. And it's fun to be creative.

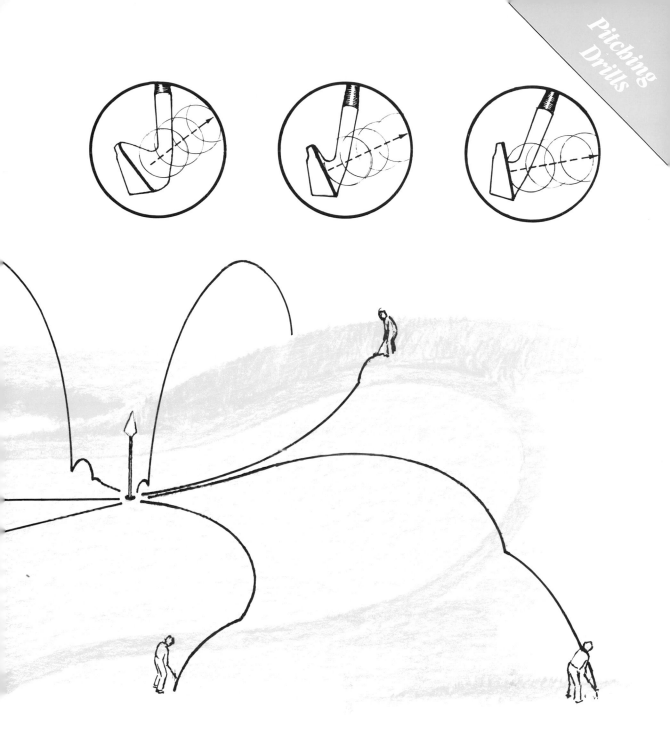

Special Pitches

One of the many fascinations of golf is that no two shots are quite the same. You can commit to muscle memory the basic pitching swing, but you always must be ready to use your imagination in dealing with specific shotmaking situations.

In this chapter I'll cover the most common special pitches: the lob shot over a bunker, the pitch and run, the low punch shot and several more. Based on that instruction, I think you can play most any shot you encounter on the course, but you'll have to be prepared to modify my advice based on the circumstances; you'll have to invent an occasional trouble shot. That's stimulating stuff—the creative aspect of the sport.

On the ninth hole at Firestone one year during a practice round for the World Series of Golf, I faced a shot I couldn't figure how to handle. I was only 30 feet from the pin, but there was a right-to-left sideslope and then a downslope to the hole. If I hit the ball short to the sideslope, it bounced too far left. If I carried the ball onto the downslope, it went way past the hole. There was no in-between shot. And if I tried to run it up through the fringe, the speed had to be perfect coming out onto the green—and the chances of bringing that off were 1 in 20.

I practiced the shot for ten minutes with a pitching wedge and couldn't get the ball within five feet of the hole. I went to the sand wedge, played a conventional shot and still couldn't get it close with 20 balls. Finally I thought to lay the face of the sand wedge wide open, take a full swing and pop the ball almost straight into the air. That balloon shot I contrived at Firestone saved me at least a couple of strokes that week, and I'll start this chapter by showing you how to hit the lob shot and this lively variation of it.

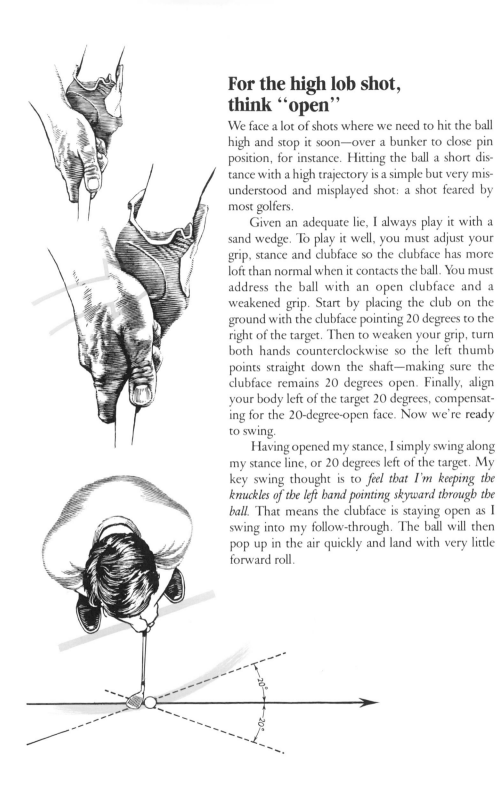

For the high lob shot, think "open"

We face a lot of shots where we need to hit the ball high and stop it soon—over a bunker to close pin position, for instance. Hitting the ball a short distance with a high trajectory is a simple but very misunderstood and misplayed shot: a shot feared by most golfers.

Given an adequate lie, I always play it with a sand wedge. To play it well, you must adjust your grip, stance and clubface so the clubface has more loft than normal when it contacts the ball. You must address the ball with an open clubface and a weakened grip. Start by placing the club on the ground with the clubface pointing 20 degrees to the right of the target. Then to weaken your grip, turn both hands counterclockwise so the left thumb points straight down the shaft—making sure the clubface remains 20 degrees open. Finally, align your body left of the target 20 degrees, compensating for the 20-degree-open face. Now we're ready to swing.

Having opened my stance, I simply swing along my stance line, or 20 degrees left of the target. My key swing thought is to *feel that I'm keeping the knuckles of the left hand pointing skyward through the ball.* That means the clubface is staying open as I swing into my follow-through. The ball will then pop up in the air quickly and land with very little forward roll.

YES

NO

125

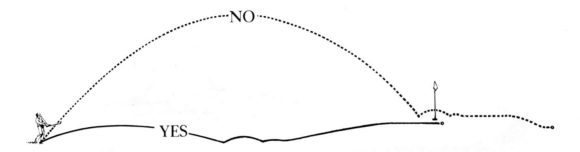

The pitch and run

This is a shot you typically need when the pin is on the back of a two-level green and you don't think you can pitch the ball onto that second level and hold the green, or when you have to run the ball onto the green because the pin's in the front and the green is hard. I prefer to land the ball on the green rather than short, particularly if the course is soft, but sometimes you have no choice.

In either case, you want to break the shot down into two parts: one in the air and the other on the ground. Picking a landing spot is critical, the same as it is in chipping. You want to land the ball on the smoothest, flattest ground possible, so it will bounce and roll predictably.

I will normally use a 9-iron or 8-iron for this shot, and set up and play it the same way I do a chip shot.

The quick-stopping punch shot

Occasionally you have to play a low shot under a tree limb, yet land and stop the ball on the green. This is one of the rare cases when I *want* spin on the shot. For you to have a chance to spin the ball, it must be lying in a relatively good lie. From heavy rough, you can't put enough spin on the ball. You must have plenty of green to work with. No matter how much spin you put on the ball, the low-flying shot will run farther than a high pitch.

To get maximum spin, select a 9-iron, pitching wedge or sand wedge. Play the ball back in your stance, back of center. Set your weight more on your left side and keep it there during the swing. This combination of ball position and weight distribution delofts the clubface and ensures a steeper swing arc into the ball. Make sure you hit the ball first, then drive the clubhead low toward the target. This keeps the ball down and imparts the backspin that will stop it on the putting surface.

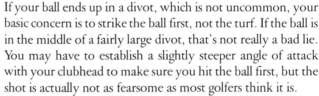

The pitch from a divot

If your ball ends up in a divot, which is not uncommon, your basic concern is to strike the ball first, not the turf. If the ball is in the middle of a fairly large divot, that's not really a bad lie. You may have to establish a slightly steeper angle of attack with your clubhead to make sure you hit the ball first, but the shot is actually not as fearsome as most golfers think it is.

It's when the ball is resting against the *back* of a divot that the trouble begins. Then the shot becomes similar to the escape from heavy rough, especially if you are some distance from the green. Set your weight left, position the ball no farther forward than the middle of your stance, lift the club up more sharply and swing into the ball at a steeper angle. Make sure you strike the ball first while the club is still travelling downward. You may catch the ball a little thin, but at least it will come out and travel a good distance, whereas striking the turf behind it will give you just a little blooper.

If the ball is resting against the front of a divot, especially a deep one, you're practically dead. Use a normal swing, but remember that the ball is going to pop high in the air. It also can ricochet sideways depending on which way the divot's pointing. If the ball's in a deep divot you can hurt yourself. In this situation just get the ball out the best way you can without damaging anything other than your score on the hole.

The pitch off hardpan

The pitch shot off hardpan is not as difficult as most golfers think. I much prefer it to a shot from heavy rough, for example. From hardpan, you can usually put a lot of spin on the ball and stop it, provided you execute the shot properly.

Just as it was on the divot shot, striking the ball first is important because you don't have nearly as much margin for error off hardpan as you do with the cushion of a normal grassy lie. As further insurance, I suggest you use a pitching wedge, rather than a sand wedge, aiming the blade squarely at your target. The more rounded flange or "bounce" of a sand wedge will cause you to blade or skull the ball from a bare lie. The pitching wedge, which has no bounce, will slide under the ball.

Your setup should be similar to the one you use for a low punch shot. The ball doesn't have to be positioned drastically back in your stance, but it should be played slightly more toward the right foot than for a pitch from a good lie. This ensures that your hands are positioned ahead of the clubhead.

Your weight should be kept slightly more on your left side, which further increases your chances of contacting the ball first. Then just make your normal swing, keeping your left hand leading down and through the ball.

The pitch from heavy rough

To play this shot I rely on one swing thought in particular: steepen the arc of the clubhead. If your angle of attack is too shallow at impact (as in a normal good swing), the heavy grass will slow or even stop the clubface. You must steepen your angle of attack so less grass gets between the clubhead and the ball at impact.

To steepen my arc, I lift the club (again, I use a sand wedge) up with my arms rather than sweep it away low on the backswing. That automatically increases the steepness of the clubhead arc on the downswing and makes for better contact in heavy rough.

Like the lob shot, I play this shot with an open clubface and stance. The only difference is that I position the ball slightly farther back in my stance from a bad lie.

Remember that a ball hit from a bad lie will roll more after it lands on the green, so allow for it.

130

The pitch from loose sand

Often there will be loose sand spilled just outside a bunker, and sometimes your ball ends up in it. This shot can be played two different ways, depending on the lie.

If the ball is sitting up well, I prefer to contact the ball first. Set your weight slightly left and play the ball slightly farther back in your stance than normal. Use a pitching wedge or 9-iron and aim your blade squarely at the target. Then make sure your left hand leads the clubhead all the way through the shot. (Never "release" and let the right hand cross the left.) Using this method you will usually catch the ball a little thin or even skull it, but that's better than a "fat" shot, which causes the ball to come up well short.

From a bad or semi-buried lie in loose sand outside the bunker, simply play a sand shot with a sand wedge. You'll learn more about this in the next chapter.

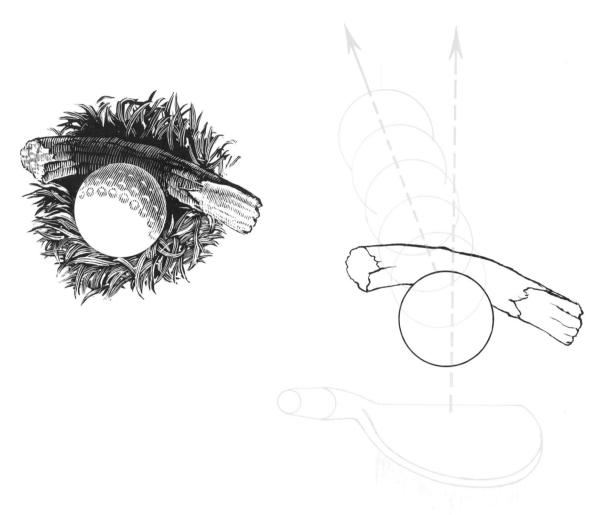

The pitch from against a stick

Occasionally your ball will come to rest against a fairly large stick, and you don't feel you can move the stick because the ball may move. Let's assume the stick is in front of the ball—if it's behind the ball, you really have a problem.

If the stick is squarely across your line of flight, the ball will come out straight, but it will fly higher and not go as far. So you have to swing harder to get to the green.

If the stick is lying at an angle, the ball will ricochet in the direction the stick is pointing. You must compensate by aiming more in the opposite direction. If the stick is pointing to the left of your target, aim to the right. You'll have to let your instincts be your guide in determining how far to the right you aim. It's a lot like a bank shot in billiards—figure the angle at which the ball is going to ricochet and aim accordingly. And remember that this shot will fly higher and shorter.

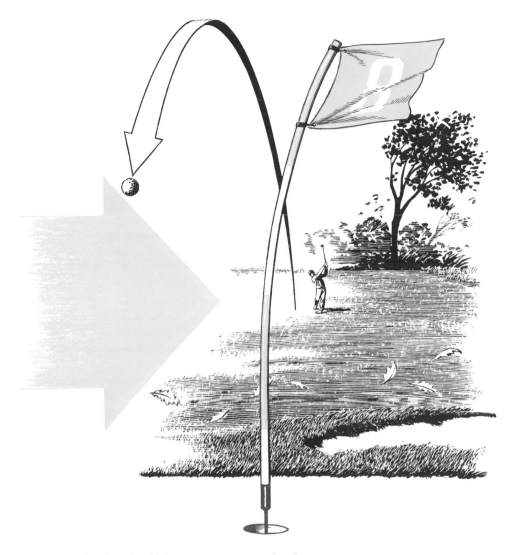

I work the ball into a crosswind

The wind can affect pitch shots more than most golfers appreciate. This is a more advanced way of playing, but in a crosswind I work the ball into the wind to keep it straight, and recommend that you do too if you have the capability to hook and slice the ball on call. With a hard right to left wind, you almost have to slice the ball to fit it into a tight green.

If you hit the ball straight and let the wind move it, on the other hand, you have a very small target area, because if the ground is hard the ball is going to land at an angle and run off the green. That's why the tour pros prefer soft conditions.

Backspin— and why I avoid it

Most fans who watch golf on television wonder how to play the half-wedge shot that screeches to a stop on the green and sucks back as if somebody pulled a string on it. Lee Trevino's a master at it. He grew up playing on hard fairways in Texas where you almost have to play that little skip shot.

Personally, I don't like to play the shot and don't recommend it because of its unpredictability. Lee is talented and experienced enough to bring it off. Not many others are. I'll play a shot like this once in a great while off hardpan, when there's really no choice, but only then.

If you want to try to play it, put the ball in the back of your stance, make a short and firm swing, and hit down hard on the ball— *bang!* If you catch the ball just right, you'll impart a lot of backspin.

Basically, backspin is simply a result of hitting the ball solidly. Every ball that gets airborne has backspin of some degree. (A flyer is a ball that has less backspin and a more parabolic flight.) That answer usually doesn't satisfy people, so I add that by positioning the ball in the back half of the stance there's more chance of putting backspin on it—but the ball will fly lower, with added forward momentum. Many times by trying to put extra backspin on the ball I don't get the desired result because just a slight mis-hit or grass between the clubface and ball at impact eliminates some of the backspin, and I hit the ball well past the hole because it doesn't check. *Bogey!*

134

Sand

Basic Sand Play

Picking the pivotal shot in a major championship isn't easy, but no shot was more important to me at Augusta when I won the 1981 Masters than the bunker shot on 17 the final day. I won't soon forget it.

Jack Nicklaus was playing just ahead of me, and he had birdied 15 and 16 to cut my lead to two strokes. If I failed to hold par at 17 and he birdied 18, we would be tied.

It was a difficult long, uphill bunker shot. The key was not to take too much sand. More about the technique later. I hit an excellent shot and it stopped about four feet to the right of the hole. I made the putt, and I knew then I would win my second green jacket.

It wasn't the first time I saved a lot more than par with my sand play, and I'm sure it won't be the last. What I want to do in this chapter is give you insight into my basic sand technique, then in the next chapter get into some of the specialty shots that you encounter so frequently: buried lies, uphill and downhill lies, the long bunker shot...

The sand stroke

In this chapter we'll put together the mechanics of a sound stroke that can make the sand shot one of the easiest recoveries in the game instead of one of the most feared. I use a weakened grip, and set up with the clubface and my body open to the target. Then I simply swing along my stance line and skip the club through the sand, keeping my left arm moving into a full, high follow-through.

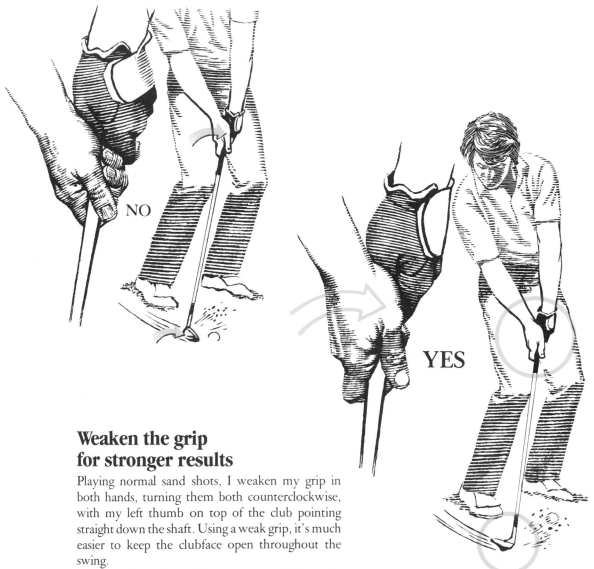

Weaken the grip
for stronger results

Playing normal sand shots, I weaken my grip in
both hands, turning them both counterclockwise,
with my left thumb on top of the club pointing
straight down the shaft. Using a weak grip, it's much
easier to keep the clubface open throughout the
swing.

A lot of you play with strong grips, which can be
fine for helping a slice and getting more distance off
the tee. In the sand, though, you will do well to
weaken your grip. If you use a strong grip, the clubface will tend to dig into, rather than skip through,
the sand, causing a variety of poor shots.

140

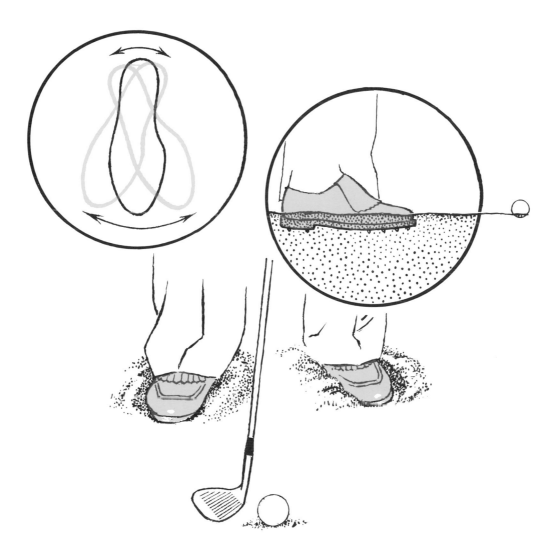

Twist your feet into the sand

You need good footing in the sand, especially if the sand is soft or sugary. The average player doesn't work his feet into the sand vigorously enough. Then playing the shot he slides around and loses his balance, making a bad shot very probable. You have to twist your feet into the sand until the movement of your feet is restricted. In soft sand, I'll twist my feet in until the sand is well above the soles of my shoes.

Remember that when you dig your feet in, your hands will be closer to the ball, so grip down nearer the shaft, which makes the club shorter, to maintain a full extension of the left arm.

Open the clubface and your body

For the basic bunker shot, I work my feet into the sand and open everything somewhat—clubface, stance, hips, shoulders—everything. I'm aligned 30 degrees left with my weight more on my left foot. Then I just swing where my body is aiming.

I'm actually swinging left of the target, but, with the clubface about 30 degrees open so that it's aimed to the right of the target, the ball goes straight at the hole. The open face affords extra loft that lets the club bounce even better through the sand. The more you open the face, the less it will dig in—you can open it 60 degrees or more and still get the ball out.

Be careful of your ball position when you pull back your left foot and open your stance in the sand. It's easy to be fooled into thinking that you have the ball too far forward, when actually you're just turning your body to the left. The ball is only two or three inches forward of center in my stance. That's why I wanted to show the setup here from an overhead view as well as from ground level.

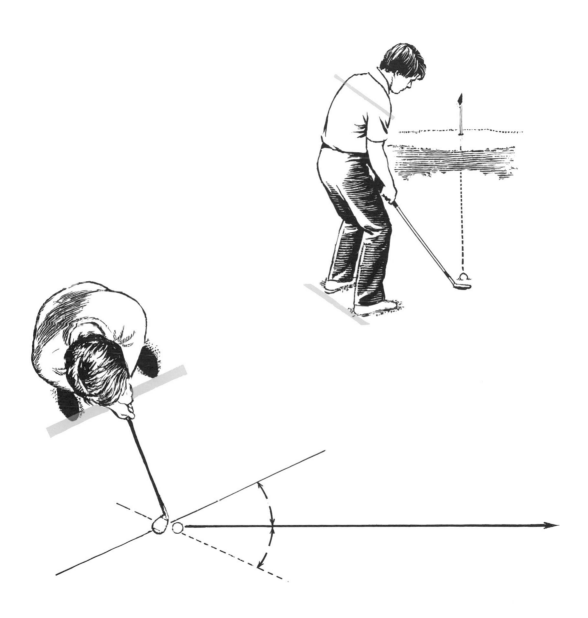

Skip the wedge through the sand

If it had been up to me, I never would have legalized the sand wedge. It makes the game a bit too easy. To a pro, most of the time it's much better to be in a bunker than in heavy rough—especially if it's the U.S. Open.

The most important thing for weekend players is to *own* a sand wedge. I'm always amazed at how many of my pro-am partners don't carry one. The construction of the club is uniquely suited to the job it has to do. The bounce—which is created because the back of the sole is closer to the ground than the leading edge—enables the club to ride through the sand without digging in. You can hit anywhere from one to three inches behind the ball and the club skips through the sand, producing the desired result. It's like a rock skipping off water.

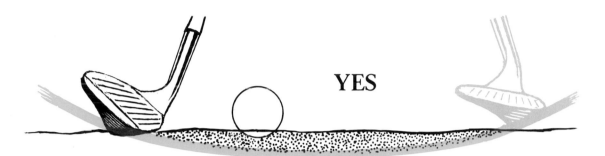

YES

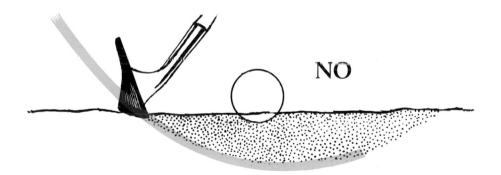

NO

The perfect divot

An ideal divot for a normal sand shot is long and shallow—longer and shallower than most players ever envision. You can enter the sand anywhere from an inch to three or four inches behind the ball, and the divot should extend through the ball eight to ten inches....at least eight inches. If you keep the face of the club open, you'll produce a long, shallow divot; the club won't dig in. A square or closed face, on the other hand, will dig in too much and produce a short, deep divot, burying the clubhead.

Picture a long and shallow divot on uphill and downhill bunker shots as well as on a level lie. A good practice idea is to go into the bunker without a ball and just work on taking long, shallow swaths out of the sand. Watch, by the way, the spot at which you want the club to enter the sand—not the ball.

Keep the left arm moving through

That poor divot we looked at—the short, deep one—is largely the result of "scooping" at the ball too much with the right hand. You have to keep the left arm moving through the shot. When I was a youngster, the only thing I was taught about sand shots was to follow through and finish high. It was solid advice.

Control distance from sand through swing length

On sand shots from around the green, most golfers have far more trouble controlling distance than direction. On a level sand shot, I prefer to control distance by simply varying the length of my swing, which is what I'd do on normal pitch shots from grass. For more distance I simply increase my arm speed by increasing my swing length.

If I let the length of my swing determine the distance the ball flies, I can swing at my normal rhythm and pace from shot to shot. This would be impossible if I were to swing harder or easier, faster or slower, on shots of different lengths. The best way to make myself hit the ball the correct length on a given shot is to concentrate on swinging at my normal rhythm and pace.

I will modify this approach slightly if the flagstick is a bit beyond my normal range or especially close to me.

The U swing vs. the V swing

My normal sand path is in the shape of a U. When I have to get the ball up quickly and land it softly, my path takes the shape of a V. At Winged Foot, the venue of the 1984 U.S. Open, a player is faced with this kind of bunker shot all the time.

In deep bunkers like those, I'll open the clubface even more than usual and lift the club up abruptly with my arms. My wrists break as I lift the club up, then release the clubhead with a steep descending blow through impact that slices under the ball and produces a short, high shot. When confronted with this type of shot, think of the V swing.

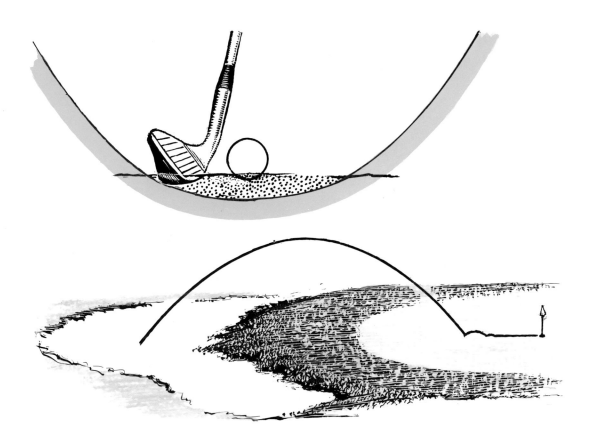

148

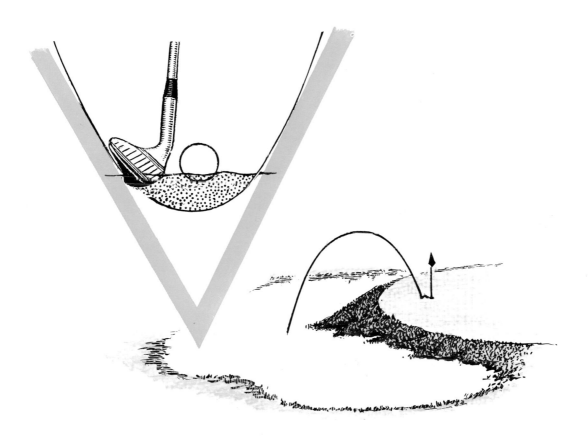

MENTAL TIP

Sand shots are probably the most feared by the weekend golfer because they're the least understood and least practiced. Let's take the fear out of them with a new attitude.

Think of the sand as your ally. If you open the face of your sand wedge and finish your swing, the ball will always come out of the bunker. You have a greater margin for error in the sand than anywhere else because you don't have to hit the ball—you only have to hit the sand an inch to three inches behind it.

The board drill

The Golf Digest *Instruction
School teachers swear by this one,
which gives you the feeling of the
club skipping through the sand.
Place a board in the practice bunker
and cover it with a couple of inches
of sand. Set a ball down and just
hit behind it with an open face. The
bounce on the club will propel it
through the sand without digging
and fly the ball out of the bunker
with ease.*

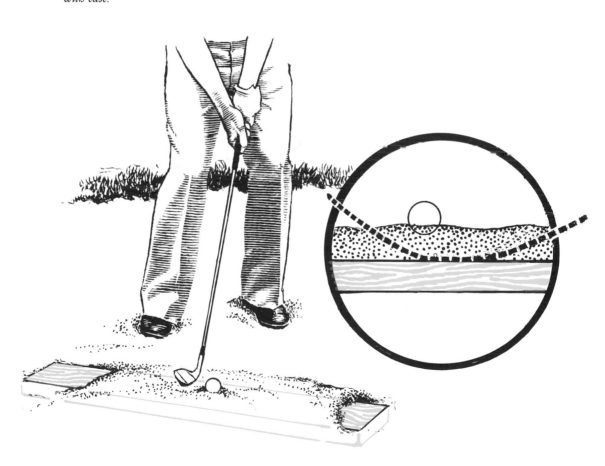

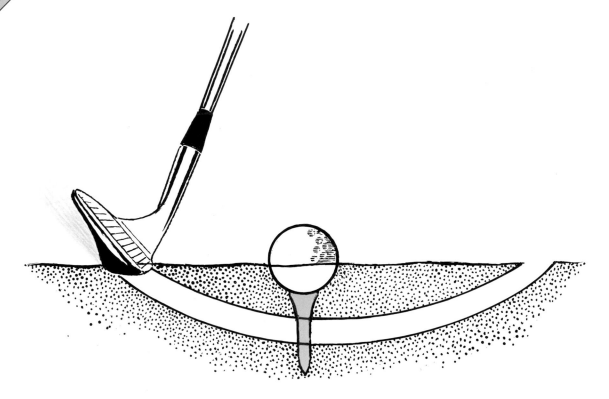

The tee drill

This teaches you to slice the club through the sand underneath the ball. Put the ball on a tee and push the tee down into the sand. Then try to clip the tee out of the sand with the leading edge of the clubface. Take a long and shallow swath of sand and keep your left arm moving through.

Special Sand Shots

Stan Thirsk, who helped me develop my game when I was younger, calls them junk shots. I used to go into a practice bunker at Kansas City C.C. and put the ball in as many different lies as I could think of, including the worst possible ones. That's how I became a good sand player. It was fun learning to recover from poor lies.

Given a basic bunker game, the overriding key to getting out of unusual lies is to *swing along the contour of the sand*. You have to swing with the slope, aligning your body perpendicular to the contour of the sand.

Unless you adjust your stance, you are going to be out of balance on these problem shots. You must put yourself in a balanced position that you can maintain as you swing. In other words, you turn an abnormal situation into a normal one insofar as you can. Picture yourself on level ground and envision what you would need to do to take a normal, shallow divot.

Practice all the lies. I do any time I go to a tournament. There's no bigger confidence builder than to make a "sandie" at an important stage of your round; it picks up your whole game.

Uphill Lie

This is probably the most misunderstood shot in the game. Golfers treat it like a normal shot and usually stick the club in the upslope, leaving the ball well short of the target. When you address the ball, it's natural to lean into the hill.

Instead, I try to *align my body with the contour of the sand.* I stand with most of my weight on my right foot, which makes my right shoulder feel very low. My key thought then is to swing the club up the slope, taking a shallow swath of sand.

Unlike a normal sand shot, where I try to keep the blade open well past impact, I let my hands release—let my right hand turn over my left through the hitting area. This action makes the ball fly with a more forward trajectory rather than too vertical a trajectory. So lean back with the slope, release the clubhead, and get the ball to the hole!

Downhill lie

This shot is more difficult than the uphill shot. The idea is to swing the clubhead under the ball without hitting the ball first or bouncing the club off the sand into the ball, which is what usually happens. As for the uphill bunker shot, *I align my body with the contour of the sand,* this time with my weight on my left side and my left shoulder lower than my right. The ball is farther back in my stance, and the face of the club is slightly open.

My backswing is an abrupt lifting of the club with my arms. On the downswing I make sure to hit behind the ball and follow through down the slope of the sand with the clubhead open and staying as low as possible. The ball will come out lower.

Ball below feet

I rely on two key thoughts for this shot: bending over at the waist and staying down throughout the swing. By bending more at the waist rather than so much at the knees, you can make an upright arm swing and keep the clubface open. The tendency whenever the ball is below your feet is to raise up too soon on the downswing and blade the shot. Stay bent at the waist and you will be in a natural position to hit the shot.

Aim left, because the shot will tend to come out to the right. A drastic version of this shot is when the ball lies just inside the bunker and you must stand outside to hit it, and we'll deal with that separately.

Ball above feet

This shot requires special technique or you probably will bury the club in the sand and fail to get the ball out. Do basically the opposite of what you would do with the ball below your feet. Stand up straighter, choke down on the grip so your arms are still extended, aim to the right because the ball tends to come out left, open the clubface slightly and be sure to follow through.

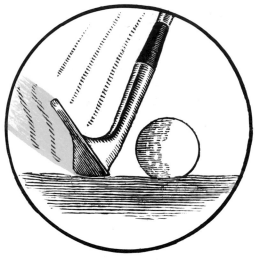

Wet or hard sand

The tendency is to bounce the flange of the club into the ball and blade it. To prevent that from happening, I put the ball more in the middle of my stance, square up the blade and hit closer to the ball with a more V-shaped swing path.

If I'm unable to work my feet into the sand, I know it's extra firm. If the ball's sitting up and there's not much of a lip on the bunker, I will chip or even putt the ball. Play the chip shot the same way you play the shot out of loose sand outside the bunker. The important thing then is to make a short, firm swing and catch the ball cleanly.

Buried lie

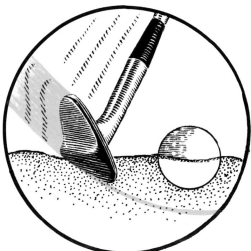

This is one shot you usually play with the clubface square or closed. The reason is to get the bottom of the clubhead underneath the ball. This forces a cushion of sand to lift the ball up and out of the buried lie. The clubhead must therefore be sharply descending into the sand just behind the ball, rather than taking a normal, shallow divot. Many times you will actually leave the clubhead in the sand. The ball comes out with no backspin, like a knuckleball, so allow for extra roll.

For a short shot with the ball partially buried, I will use a pitching wedge or 9-iron, open the clubface slightly, lift the club up abruptly, and hit just behind the ball with a sharply descending blow. The club finishes low and to the left of my left foot. The ball pops up and out softly with a minimum of roll.

On a long buried shot, I might play a 9-iron or even an 8-iron and go ahead and hit behind the ball with a square face.

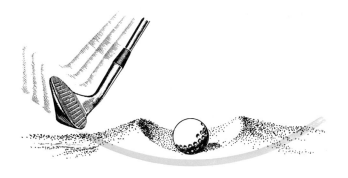

Fried egg

This shot gets its name from its appearance, and it's no breakfast special. It's a very difficult lie because you have sand to go through, then no sand, then more sand. The most important factor is to recognize how far the ball is below the level of the sand. You must be sure to work the leading edge of your sand wedge underneath the ball with a square or closed face and force a cushion of sand to lift the ball out of the lie.

Ball in a footprint

We all know what should be done to golfers who don't rake their footprints after they play out of a bunker, and we know it's hard to get through a casual round without facing this shot. My fundamental thought as for any buried bunker shot is to swing the leading edge of the club just underneath the ball.

I vary the steepness of my swing arc and open or close the clubface depending on where the ball is in the footprint and how far it is below the surface level of the sand. Sometimes I play it like a buried bunker shot and close the blade, if I have a lot of sand to swing through to get the leading edge under the ball. Other times I'll pick the clubhead up more, with an open blade, if I have a clear path to the ball but it's below the level of the sand.

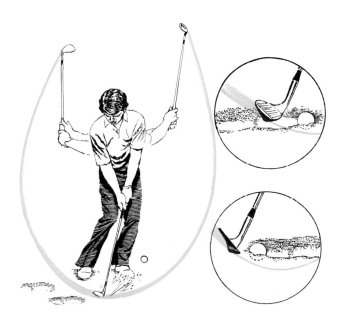

Ball in bunker, golfer outside

With the ball well below your feet here, you have to bend over more at the waist to address it, which makes it difficult to swing the club. In this position you're out of balance to start with, and you need to do everything possible to retain what balance you have.

Make the club as long as you can by gripping to the very end. Open the clubface slightly, then swing more with the arms and restrict your body movement, staying in the same bent-over position throughout the swing. If you bob your head up and down—the prevalent tendency—you're going to miss the shot. Aim left, since the ball will tend to fly to the right.

Golfer in bunker, ball outside

This is a shot I've had to play many times at the Tournament Players Championship because the faces of most of the bunkers are nearly vertical. The first thing you have to do is make the club shorter. A lot of times you'll have to grip down with both hands on the steel. I've played this shot making the club only a foot long; I couldn't stay in balance any other way.

When the ball's up around your waist, aim well right of the target and position the ball back in your stance. Swing your arms back and through, making sure you lead the clubhead through the impact zone with your hands well ahead of the ball. This action will start the ball on line. If you release the clubhead at all with your hands, you will pull the ball well left of your target.

Ball under side lip

Here's a not-so-unusual situation that comes up more often in Britain, where the lips of the bunkers are more vertical. You hit into the left side of a deep bunker so that you can't take any sort of stance; you can't bend over far enough.

When I face this shot, I put my right foot in the bunker and play off the knee of my left leg. My left knee's up on the lip, my right foot's in the sand behind the ball. Now I can extend down to the ball, making the shot relatively easy. Sometimes I've even played the shot off both knees.

YES

Ball plugged under front lip

I set up with my weight on my right side, braced against the slope. I lean back with my upper body so that I can swing up the slope. As for any buried bunker shot, I try to swing the leading edge of the clubhead just underneath the ball. I usually open the clubface slightly, but if the ball is very close to the lip I'll open it more and swing harder. The deeper the ball is buried, the greater a test of strength this shot becomes.

The long, 40-yard bunker shot

If I have a bunker shot of 40 yards or more, which I consider one of the toughest shots in golf, I square up the blade, play the ball in the middle of my stance and swing a little harder, allowing my hands and the clubhead to "release" as they do on the uphill shot. For very long bunker shots, say over 40 yards, I would consider using a pitching wedge, or even a 9-iron or 8-iron, and just hitting an inch behind the ball. This is a shot you must practice to learn the right feel for distance.

Practice

My twofold objective in this book was to teach you fundamentals and then give you enjoyable, imaginative drills to make them instinctive. If you don't know and use the basic fundamentals, you cannot learn or be taught a *consistent* short game. You will always be erratic and have problems.

If you don't practice and do drills, you can never play by feel, with your mind free of mechanical thoughts so you can concentrate on the specific situation at hand. The short game requires more understanding and practice than the long game. If you're a beginner or high handicapper, you certainly shouldn't worry about the long swings until you've grasped the ultimate purpose of the game: to get the ball into the hole. You do that with your short game.

Once you've learned to putt the ball, then to chip it and then to pitch it, you're ready for the full swing, which is essentially just a longer version of the chipping and pitching strokes. The best way of developing your full golf swing is to work from mini-swings up, rather than the other way around, and once you begin to master the short game it's merely a matter of time until you master the long game.

To me, practice is enjoyable and rewarding. I get great satisfaction out of hitting good shots. I often play competitive little games against myself to keep practice from becoming dull. I'll try to get up and down out of a difficult uphill bunker lie eight times out of ten, for example. I designed many of these drills in contest form to keep up your interest in practicing.

Practice with purpose

I suppose no one has ever practiced as rigorously as Ben Hogan, who was a self-taught player. If he wasn't competing in a tournament he'd practice eight hours a day, seven days a week. He'd try to hit a bucket of balls with every club, starting up against the green and working back to his long power fade with a driver. He worked on every conceivable little recovery shot, because he never wanted to hit a shot in a tournament that he hadn't practiced.

When I practice, I practice with a purpose. I work on a change in feel, my address position, whatever. I hit every shot with a specific intent. That's one secret of Jack Nicklaus' greatness: *he seems never to hit a practice shot that he doesn't take as seriously as a shot on the last hole of a major championship.* He's never careless with a practice shot, never hits balls without a purpose.

I know you have much less time to practice than I do. Golf is my full-time job. If you're a weekend golfer with a busy job, I encourage you to spend thirty minutes a couple of evenings a week concentrating on your short game. This can improve your scoring dramatically. Practice sand shots and other trouble shots as well as standard putts and chips. If you have an hour, spend at least half of it on your short game; I'd recommend forty-five minutes on the short game and fifteen minutes on the long game.

There are other types of practice that should be part of any serious improvement program.

Practice with a teacher

This should be your first step in learning the fundamentals and establishing a good base. Give serious consideration to taking short game lessons. Most golfers never think of going to a teacher for help with anything except the full swing. A lesson or two on the short game can result in much faster improvement in your scoring.

Otherwise I like to practice alone, so I can concentrate fully, but if I'm having a problem I like to have someone whose knowledge I respect watch me. I'll ask my father, Stan Thirsk (the head professional at the Kansas City Country Club) or Byron Nelson if they will watch me while I hit balls. I'll hit a few and ask them what they think before I volunteer what I'm trying to do, so I don't prejudice them.

I think it's a mistake to solicit help from a dozen sources. I go to a few people who know my game and can spot a difference when I'm doing something wrong. A friend who's played with you for a long time and who's a student of the game could serve you in the same way. You can get very confused if you start listening to a lot of different teachers (or, for that matter, read a lot of different books). The differences in their terminology alone can mix you up; Ben Crenshaw said that's a difficulty he had when he was in a slump a couple of years ago. Jack Nicklaus has been taught almost exclusively by Jack Grout since he started playing at age ten.

Pre-round practice

I usually arrive at the course about an hour before my tee time and relax in the locker room for a few minutes before I go out to practice. I'll do a few stretching exercises because the older I get, the less limber I am. I wish I had my wife Linda's flexibility; she's as limber as Sam Snead.

Then I go out and warm up for thirty-five minutes, the first twenty on the range and the second fifteen on the practice putting green. I'll start with short wedge shots on the range and work up to the driver, checking my fundamentals and feel of the club. Yes, my feel of the club usually changes from day to day when I first swing. After fine-tuning my tempo and feel of the day, I go to the practice green and putt (with three balls) a variety of putts: uphill, downhill, left-right, right-left, two-footers and sixty-footers. Mainly I'm trying to get a feel for the speed of the greens.

Finally I chip a few balls to get the feel of the fringe and rough around the green and try to see how the ball bounces and rolls on the green. If I have time, I'll chip with different clubs to get a feel for the variety of shots I might face on the course.

I include sand shots in my pre-round warmup if there's a practice bunker. I want to know how fast or slow the ball's coming out of the sand before I get onto the course, especially if the course conditions have changed from the day before—due to a heavy rain, for example.

If I were to arrive at the course late, the way weekend players often do, with only a few minutes to warm up, I'd spend them stretching first and then on the practice green, particularly if I'd never played the course. If the greens are fast, you urgently need to get a feel for the speed, or your round could start disastrously and be ruined after the first two or three holes.

Post-round practice

The most valuable time to practice is right after your round, when your mistakes are fresh in your mind. Replaying the strengths and weaknesses

of a round on the practice tee immediately after finishing play is a good discipline and excellent learning tool. I like to correct a pattern of poor shots as soon as I can. If I had trouble with short left-to-right putts and a particular bunker shot, I might putt a hundred left-to-right putts until I find the problem and then go to the practice bunker and try to solve that problem as well.

I usually spend more time practicing after a round than I do before. Before the round, I'm just warming up the engine. After the round, I'm making repairs and fine-tuning the engine. It's a good way to wind down. Many times I can work out a problem I was having, which gives me a boost of confidence for the next round. And I sleep better that night.

Indoor practice

If you live in a seasonal climate, a little practice around the house during the off-season—or on inclement weekends—can be a great help in developing and retaining your fundamentals and feel. The short game is the hardest part of golf to recapture after a layoff, but you can keep it in tune by doing a few drills indoors.

Putting the ball on a smooth carpet isn't like putting on an undulating green, but it's a good way to make your stroke more consistent. A rug does have grain in it, the same as grass, and you can develop a better feel for the effect of grain.

I like to chip the ball off the carpet. You have to be careful to practice away from breakables, however. I learned that the hard way one day—by breaking a full bottle of wine.

No matter where or when you work on your short game, practice doesn't have to be tedious. Use the drills and play competitive games against yourself, and you'll make your practice fun as well as productive.

Equipment

The best fundamentals in the world won't help you if your equipment doesn't fit you. I've spent hundreds of hours testing different clubs to find what's best for me. My equipment isn't necessarily what's best for you, but I think I've learned some basic guidelines that can help you.

Most golfers will buy a driver or a basic set of irons and pay special attention to the specifications they need, but rarely will they concern themselves enough with the "scoring" clubs: the putter and the sand and pitching wedges. Even your regular set of irons should be selected with chipping and pitching in mind: you'll probably use your 5-iron through 9-iron as much for little shots around the green as for full shots.

The three-wedge concept

The short game should also influence the composition of the fourteen clubs in your bag. I recommend that weekend players use *three wedges*, though I don't use three myself. I get enough value from my 2-iron to justify carrying it, but the average player would be better off leaving the 2-iron out of his bag and adding a third wedge. If you carry a driver, 3-wood and 5-wood, you can hit the 5-wood a lot easier than you can a 2-iron, with comparable results.

Tom Kite and an increasing number of pros play the tour with three wedges. Tom has the loft of his long irons adjusted so they're in between the normal club numbers: his 3-iron is actually a 2¹/₂-iron, his 4-iron a 3¹/₂-iron. That way he is able to eliminate a long iron and add a 60-degree wedge for playing shorter and middle-distance pitch shots with a fuller, harder swing. While I haven't gone to the three-wedge concept, I *have* increased the loft of my sand wedge from 56 to 58 degrees, making it more effective as an all-round weapon, both in the bunker and around the green.

A pitching wedge is normally 51 to 52 degrees and a sand wedge 56. If you add a third, 60-degree wedge, you can hit the ball much higher, which most golfers have trouble doing on short shots. You don't have to open the face or lay it back or set your hands behind the ball; you just swing normally and the ball gets up in the air naturally.

I can hit the ball with my sand wedge a maximum of about 100 yards in the air. Your maximum might be more like 60 yards. I can hit the ball with a 60-degree wedge about 80 yards. Your maximum might be more like 40 yards, that risky distance we dealt with in the pitching chapter. With a pitching wedge or sand wedge, you have to make a more difficult partial or half swing from 40 yards. With a 60-degree wedge, you can make a full swing or something close to it, which is simply easier to execute than the half swing.

A third wedge of 60-degree loft also can come in handy on shorter shots when you need to hit the ball up in the air quickly and land it softly, lobbing it over a bunker to a tight pin position, for example. Or on pitching the ball a short distance out of the rough, when you can't get any spin on the ball and it's difficult to stop after it lands.

The sand wedge

The overriding consideration with this club is simply to be sure you own one. It's the best trouble club there is, and not just in the sand. More than any other, this club gives you a built-in advantage for playing the challenging high lob shot. I wish it had been called a trouble wedge rather than a sand wedge.

Do you know the difference between a pitching wedge and a sand wedge? The typical sand wedge is designed so that the back of the sole rests on the ground with the leading edge at varying heights above the ground. This allows the club to slide through the sand without digging. This sole configuration is called the sand wedge's "bounce."

I'm not an advocate of a lot of bounce in my own sand wedge because then the club isn't very adaptable to hard sand or off hard, bare turf. But a sand wedge must have bounce to be effective, and yours may need more or less than mine. If you lay the face of the club open, you increase the bounce and make it more difficult for the clubhead to dig too much into the sand or turf.

The conditions at your home course could be a factor in how much bounce you want on your sand wedge. If the sand in your bunkers is soft, you can use a lot of bounce. If it's hard, you want less bounce. If you add a third wedge to your set, you might prefer more bounce in your sand wedge and a surer chance of getting out of any bunker.

Now a critical, critical point, in my view. Most sand wedges, because of their big, thick metal flanges, are quite heavy—*too heavy*. I recommend light to medium weight. My irons are swingweighted D-3, and my sand wedge is just slightly heavier at D-5. That's a difference of only two dollar bills when calculating the swingweight. The heavier the clubhead, the harder it is to control it. You have to swing more slowly, and that's not easy for the average player when he's facing a shot that makes him uncomfortable to start with. Another reason not to use a heavy-headed sand wedge is because it will feel much different from the other clubs in your bag when it really should feel the same.

With a light wedge, you can control the clubhead much better. It's difficult to find a light one, but you can take your wedge to a pro or to a club repair shop and have weight removed from the back of the flange. Some better players like to own several sand wedges for varying types of sand and turf conditions.

I like a rounded rather than straight leading edge on my sand club. When I lay the clubhead open—and I play most of my short shots with the clubface open to varying degrees—the rounded leading edge fits behind the ball closer than a straight leading edge. Optically, it gives me the feeling I can swing the leading edge just beneath the ball easier.

A rounded leading edge also makes it easier to play from a sideslope. With a straight leading edge you have a tendency to address the ball with the heel or toe of the club resting on the ground, which causes a pulled or a pushed shot. With the rounded edge you don't have that tendency as much.

Chipping and pitching clubs

Here too I prefer lighter clubs because they're easier to control on little touch shots.

I like a little rounded look to the sole, a little camber from toe to heel. I don't like a sharp leading edge, because if you hit the ball fat it's not going to cut through the grass as well, especially when you're playing on stiff grass like Bermuda.

Pitching wedge

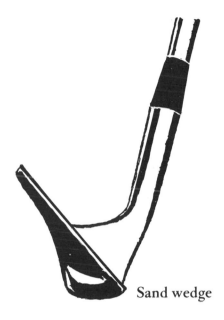

Sand wedge

Sand wedge laid open

With all iron clubs it's important to be fitted by a professional for the lie that suits your address position, so the club soles correctly. The lie is the angle between the sole of the clubhead and the shaft.

I've been asked if I recommend carrying a chipper, a specialty club designed for chipping. I don't, because I think you face too many different shots around the green to handle them with one club—that's the same reasoning I gave in opposing the idea of chipping with only one club. I think you limit the development of your game. A chipper can be useful for routine shots from the fringe, if you can afford to take one of the other clubs out of your bag to make room for it. But if it comes down to a choice between a chipper and a third wedge, I'd rather see you carry a third wedge.

The putter

Here's your most important club—the weapon that can make up for any number of mistakes from tee to green.

The putter must have smooth, rounded edges so you don't catch the grass on your takeaway or follow-through. That's the first thing.

I favor a grip that's flat on top, because I want both thumbs pointing down the top of the shaft. I like an offset putter because it automatically puts my hands ahead of the ball at address.

I like an alignment line on top of the head, coinciding exactly with the location of the putter's sweet spot because I always will try to hit the ball at the sweet spot.

The lie (the angle of the sole and shaft) must fit your posture and putting technique. If you're shopping for a putter, don't adjust your putting style to a new putter—find the right putter for your style. The lie of a putter can be changed.

My putter is 35 inches long, but your style may necessitate a shorter or longer model. Andy North, who's a six foot four former basketball player, bends so far over to putt that he has to use a shorter-than-standard putter. Andy makes more of an arm-and-shoulder stroke with less wrist action; his left wrist stays firm through impact, which is good. The putterhead stays very low to the ground, back and through. The disadvantage is that you must use more effort to hit the ball a given distance with a short putter that with a long putter.

A longer-than-standard putter, on the other hand, requires less effort, and tends to swing by itself. Raymond Floyd, for example, uses a longer putter. But a longer putter can cause extension problems with the elbows, which we discussed during the first putting chapter, and can cause the left wrist to break down through the ball. Since it takes less effort to swing it, there's an unfortunate tendency to swing back too far and then decelerate at impact.

If you consistently have trouble with your putting, I'd quickly suggest trying a *heavier putter*. My putter weighs 17 ounces, which is on the heavy end of the standard range that most pros use. A number of putters weighing 20 ounces and more are on the market now, and those that are well-balanced could help a lot of people who have ongoing problems on the greens. A heavy putter forces you to swing the clubhead back and through with a slower stroke. And since there is more mass in the head, the mis-hits will tend to be better. For anyone with the yips, a heavy putter could be the cure.

The old wisdom was that you employed a light putter on fast greens and a heavy putter on slow greens. I'm not surprised that some new research indicates that a heavier putter performs better on both fast and slow greens. A poor putter has to do better with a heavier club.

If you like the looks of your old, battered putter but want more weight, you can apply lead tape to the back of the putterhead. Some pros do that when they come to a course with slow greens. Most home professionals have rolls of lead tape in their shops, and can help you apply it.

I'm not one for switching putters once I've found one that feels good and works. If I run into a streak of bad putting, it's almost certainly my stroke or confidence that's the problem, not the putter. I will very seldom change to a different putter. When I do it's almost always just for practice when I'm putting poorly. To change the feel and look with a different putter is sometimes a good idea, but don't change putters every time you have a bad putting round. That breeds indecision on the greens and is a bad habit to develop. Stick with one putter and weather the bad streaks. I don't want to have to adapt to a different putter just because the greens are faster or slower this week, either. I wouldn't change cars just because I was going on a long trip or a short trip—I'd drive the same car.

Putting Theory into Play

My Final Nine Holes of the 1982 U.S. Open

The day before the tournament started, I said you have to have a little magic in you to win the U.S. Open. I had a little in me on the 17th hole the last day when I chipped in from out of the rough. It was the greatest shot of my life and it won the championship I most wanted to win.

To win the national championship that way, in a close finish with Jack Nicklaus, the greatest player ever, on a great course like Pebble Beach, is almost too much to hope for. It fulfilled a lot of dreams. I needed a little magic, a little luck, all the skill I could muster and the best thinking I was capable of. At this level of the game, where dozens of players strike the ball and putt so well, the mental dimension is often the difference, particularly in major championships. I'll take you inside my head to share my thought processes on the last nine holes, show you why I hit every shot the way I did. I think the experience will help you play better regardless of your shotmaking ability. No matter how well you hit the ball, you have to think well to start with, have to be aware of your options and pick the right one.

I did hit the ball very well at Pebble. I missed only one fairway the final round and drove the ball farther than I ever have driven in an Open—averaging nearly 300 yards off the tee. But I won the tournament as much with my mind as with my clubs. I plotted a game plan and stuck with it Sunday on every shot except for my layup on 18. Needless to say, my short game was vital to my victory. You'll recognize over and over the absolute importance of the short game as we play our way through these nine holes.

There's no easy way to play Pebble. It's such a strong course it can leave you defenseless at times. Fortunately I've played the course enough—ever since I used to slip on at dawn as a college student at Stanford—to know where to hit the ball and where not to hit it. You have to position every shot. You have to think out every shot. You have to do that anywhere, but especially at Pebble. When it plays easy, with no wind, it can lull you to sleep. It's a thinking man's test of golf.

If I made a mistake, I made it in a favorable direction. I didn't hit many double-crosses—hooks when I was playing for fades, or vice versa. I didn't try to draw the ball on 15 and then leave it out to the right, for example. I played with Craig Stadler in the first round, and he hit it out-of-bounds that way. My misses left me with a chance to recover. Of course, if I hadn't been able to convert these chances by pitching, chipping and putting well, I would have lost.

Going into the last round, I was tied for the lead with Bill Rogers, at four under par, and I had one very good thing going for me. I had played a solid round on Saturday, a much better round than I played Thursday or Friday, and because *I was putting well* and driving exceptionally well, I had a good chance to win.

The down side of my week had been an inability to score well on the first seven holes, where you usually pick up the most birdies at Pebble, but I had made up for it by playing the tough finishing holes well. The first round I birdied 15, 16 and 17 to get back to even par, and I made birdies on the late holes Friday and Saturday. Waiting to tee off Sunday, I knew in the back of my mind that if I had a chance to win that afternoon, I could play those strong holes well. I felt I had the confidence you have to have to win the Open. I told my caddie Bruce Edwards just to keep reminding me to keep my tempo smooth.

I was paired with Rogers, a comfortable man to play with because he's pleasant and concentrates well. I almost play in a vacuum myself. I say very little and at times I'm barely aware of what is happening to my playing partner or even on the leader boards. I know when the tournament takes a dramatic turn—the crowd will make you aware that something big has happened, or your caddie does—but I'm pretty much preoccupied with my own game plan and my next shot.

I was even par on the front side, 36, and at the turn I still shared the lead with Bill at four under. Jack Nicklaus, a couple of groups ahead of us, had birdied five holes in a row and was threatening. *I had birdied the par-5 second hole by getting up and down out of the sand, then bogeyed the next hole when I hit my approach shot fat and the ball buried in the bunker.* It's funny how certain holes haunt you—I've never played No. 3 well, and I bogeyed it two of four days.

The bothersome aspect of the front nine was that I didn't hit a good, solid putt except for the 10-footer at No. 2. On the tiny seventh hole, I hit a pitching wedge about two feet from the cup—and missed the putt. I just stepped up to the ball, took the putter back a little too much outside, and pulled it. I locked up and didn't accelerate the putter through the ball. It was a missed opportunity, but there was nothing to do but put it out of mind.

The course starts getting difficult with the eighth and ninth holes, and I parred both of them, missing a good birdie chance at nine. *After that, putts began to drop.*

No. 10, 424 yards, par 4

The 10th is the tightest driving hole on the course, because the fairway slopes so drastically from left to right, toward the ocean. It widens out the longer you hit the ball, though.

I set up to hit a left-to-right tee shot, starting the ball at the left bunker and letting it run down into the heart of the fairway. I crunched the drive and had a 7-iron for my second shot. The flagstick was in the right front part of the green and *I didn't want to hit my second shot past the hole and give myself a difficult putt.* I had 155 yards to the flag, with the wind blowing from right to left and a downhill lie. I wanted to cut the 7-iron shot, but I pushed it, and it started at the flag and then cut. I wound up short and to the right of the green, down in the kikuyu grass rough in the hazard, well below the level of the green.

The kikuyu grass is stiff and the ball was sitting up, which it probably wouldn't have been in Bermuda grass or bluegrass. *It was an easier shot than it appeared to be. I hit a sand-wedge shot on the top part of the face and left the ball 25 feet short on the fringe. In retrospect, a pitching wedge would have been a smarter club selection on a severe upslope than the more lofted sand wedge.*

The putt looks as though it breaks right, but I knew from experience in past tournaments at Pebble Beach that it's dead straight. I played a straight putt, and it went straight in. Finally—my first really good putt of the day! My putter was warming up at last.

Rogers bogeyed, and my par putt put me in the lead.

No. 11, 382 yards, par 4

It's a blind driving hole over the brow of a hill, and the key is to stay left. The one fairway bunker is over there, but you can carry it fairly easily.

If you miss your drive to the right, it's a very difficult par, since you have to carry the ball from the rough over a bunker to a small target that runs away from you. You can bounce the ball onto the green from the left rough but not from the right rough.

I hit a big drive into the right side of the fairway and had only a pitching wedge to the green. I didn't hit that one well, but got it on the green and faced about a 22-foot putt that broke quite a bit from left to right.

I'm more at ease with a right-to-left putt, as most people are, but *I made a good, firm stroke and the ball went smack in the hole.* Suddenly I was two strokes ahead.

No. 12, 204 yards, par 3

If you're playing the 12th in the Crosby Pro-Am early in the year, the green will hold. In the summer it won't unless it's uncommonly soft. If the pin is on the left side of the green, where it was Sunday, you cannot stop the ball with a long iron unless you hit it toweringly high and land it dead. A wide bunker runs almost clear across the front of the green from left to right.

I tried to hit a 3-iron at the right side of the green and draw it in just a bit. I wasn't trying to draw it in to the pin, because the green slopes that way and all I needed to do was land the ball on the front right and it would roll naturally to the left and leave me with a putt of 20 or 25 feet for birdie.

I was aiming at a 20-foot landing area, and I pushed the shot and it went in the right bunker, from where *I hit a poor sand shot that was short by 15 feet. It was just a horrible sand shot.*

I didn't want to charge the putt because it was terribly fast, faster than it looked, and I had seen players three-putt from there. It curled from right to left, I didn't get it quite high enough, and it stopped just below the hole.

The bogey sent me back to four under par. I was two ahead of Rogers and very briefly one ahead of Nicklaus. Bruce reminded me to keep my tempo smooth.

No. 13, 393 yards, par 4

The sin on the hole is to be right, especially with the pin in the right front where it was Sunday. The green slopes right to left. You want to be left off the tee.

You can drive it in the left fairway bunker—or even left of the bunker—and be better off than hitting it to the right. Nicklaus drove it left of that bunker when he won the Open in 1972, had a straight shot at the right-hand pin position, and made par. If you go right, you have no shot.

I moved my hands ahead some to play the tee ball from right to left and really flushed it, 300 yards into the left side of the fairway.

With the pitching wedge, I wanted to hit the ball up into the green far enough that I would have a straight putt. If you're short or long, you have to deal with a severely breaking putt. The idea is to be hole high and a little left, because from the right of the hole it's a much faster putt with a more sweeping break.

I hit a good shot with the pitching wedge, 15 feet left of the hole, and was looking at a 15-foot, straight-in putt. I pushed it just a hair, and missed it.

About this time Nicklaus birdied 15 ahead of me, and we were tied. My adrenaline was really flowing, and I was extremely intense.

No. 14, 565 yards, par 5

This is a sharp dogleg to the right, and I slid the ball strongly off the tee. My starting point for the drive is 20 yards left of the right bunker. You can see the top of that bunker from the tee if you're five ten. Since I'm five nine, I have to jump up to find it. Then I aim left of it and work the ball from left to right.

My drive was long, but I didn't consider going for the green with my second shot. It's a small target with a big bunker in front and a big drop-off in back, and you can go out-of-bounds to either side. *You never want to go over the green on 14, because you'll be playing back to a treacherous green that slopes away from you and is terribly fast. And if you fall short into the front bunker, the ball buries.*

I laid up with a 5-iron. I wanted a full sand wedge for my third shot, and I told Bruce, my caddie, that I wanted to leave myself with a 95-yard shot. I hit a good 5-iron, with just a touch of draw, and left myself with a 96-yard shot.

The lie wasn't good. The ball was above my feet with not much of a cushion under it. I hit it thin—in fact, I cut the ball, I hit it so thin—and it went to the back fringe, 35 feet past the hole.

I asked Bruce what he thought about the putt, and he said he thought it was going to break right as it reached the hole. I agreed. I saw it breaking left at the beginning, but more right than left after that. The speed was as difficult to gauge as the line. The putt was downhill as well as curving, and I just hoped to get it close. I left the pin in as a backstop.

I played it about six inches left of the hole and popped it good and solidly. The speed was perfect and the line was perfect, and it dropped into the cup for a birdie! It was the *putt that won the tournament for me.*

And for the first time that day, the pressure wasn't pushing me. It simply left, and I felt a great inner calm. I knew what I was trying to do and was doing it, and I was enjoying myself for the first time in the round. I've been in that mental state a few times, and it's the greatest feeling you can have in golf.

The pressure was gone, I had control of the situation, the game was on. I led Jack by one, with Bill Rogers three behind. It was a two-man battle, with Jack going for a record fifth Open and me for my first. I knew it was down to a shoot-out with the greatest player of all time, and I drew on old positive memories. I thought back to the 1977 British Open at Turnberry, when I shot 65–65 the last two rounds and Jack shot 65–66.

No. 15, 395 yards, par 4

The tee points you to the right of the fairway, and the objective is to hook the ball into the left side of the fairway. Even with the pin on the left where it was, you have a better shot at it from the left rough than from the right with the trees, a bunker and OB looming over there.

I laced a tee shot perfectly up the left side of the fairway, down into the gully. From there I hit a pitching wedge just to the right of the hole, and the ball just stayed up there. I thought it would kick down but it didn't.

My putt was only about 12 or 13 feet, with a right-to-left break. *I played a bit too much break.* The ball went past the high side of the hole. A good opportunity missed, but I still had a one-shot lead with three holes to play.

No. 16, 403 yards, par 4

My close friend Frank (Sandy) Tatum, a fellow Stanford alumnus and a past president of the U.S. Golf Association, had a bunker to the right of the driving zone on 16 redesigned to be deep and heavily penal. With plenty of room on the left, that high-lipped bunker is the one place on the hole you do not want to go. Naturally I drove the ball into Frank D. Tatum Jr.'s new bunker.

The hole's only 400 yards, but I had hit a driver every day and got away with missing the ball to the right—I even made a birdie from the right bunker. Sunday I considered a 3-wood, but told myself to hit the driver at the left edge of the right bunker with a little draw and knock it on down there so I could spin a full sand wedge at the flag, which was on the front of the green. That's how you stop the ball near that pin position, and I was thinking birdie and a two-stroke lead.

Well, I started my drive at the left edge of the bunker on the dogleg-right hole, but instead of drawing, the ball tailed to the right and went in the bunker. It was the only fairway I missed all day. With the lip of the bunker hitting me at about eye level, I couldn't get the ball up quickly enough to go for the green, and my only play was to come out sideways with a sand wedge.

Architects in America don't often design bunkers this penal. The British do, using bunkers to exact a harsh penalty very much as American designers tend to use water.

I hit out of the bunker to the fairway, and left myself with a third shot off a severe downslope to a pin on the front left of the green. *I hit too far behind the ball with a sand wedge and got a flier—a shot without enough spin.* It hit in the middle of the green and went all the way to the back left edge, 50 feet beyond the hole.

Now I needed to two-putt from there just to stay even with Nicklaus. *If I hit the putt too hard, I easily could go 12 to 15 feet past the hole. And there was one more difficulty: a huge left-to-right break between me and the cup.*

It was my most difficult putt of the tournament. I played at least 10 feet of break—a tremendous break—and picked an intermediate spot to aim at. And I knocked it up stone dead, within a foot of the hole, for an ''easy'' bogey. I've never hit a better pressure putt.

I went to the 17th tee tied with Nicklaus, who had parred 17 and 18. What I had to do now was hit four good shots. I had to birdie one of the last two holes.

No. 17, 209 yards, par 3

There's just no out on 17; you either hit it on the green or you're in trouble

On the tee, which was back Sunday, I was debating between a 3-iron and 2-iron. I considered the 3 because I was very pumped up, but I went with the 2-iron because it was into the wind and the pin was on the back left of the long, two-level green. Bruce agreed it was the right club.

I'd hit good shots at 17 all week—had made two birdies and just missed another one—so I was confident. I was trying to draw the ball off the TV tower behind the green and swing it in to the pin. I started the shot at the tower, but I had come over the top of the shot, and I swung it too much. The ball landed hard to the left of the green—even if it had hit the green it would have gone over.

It rolled up where I couldn't see it, and I said to myself, *''Uh, oh, now I'm dead.'' I knew I was in the rough close to the hole, with a downhill lie, to a downhill green.* Walking up to the green, I told myself I was going to have to make a long putt to save par and that was all there was to it. I was resigned to that.

But when I got to the ball I saw I had a good lie, and it was as if the sun chose that moment to come out. I had a good feeling all over. I knew I could get the ball close enough to have a makable putt. *The ball was lying*

downhill, which would make it difficult to get it in the air quickly and land it softly, but I would be able to slide the club under the ball, and that was the key. I'd practiced dozens of little shots like this by the hour.

Bill Rogers played first because he was farther away even though he'd hit the green. I walked over to Bruce, and he was choking. He mumbled something about how I could get the ball close, and I said, "I'm not going to get the ball close —I'm going to sink it." Right then and there I honestly believed I was going to hole the shot.

I went back to the slope where my ball was. I had about 20 feet to the hole, with 12 feet of green to the pin. I took a couple of practice swings and addressed the shot. It was going to break a good foot to the right after it landed on the green, but I felt I was lined up for too much break, so I aimed a little more to the right, took one last look, and picked the club up away from the ball.

I had opened the blade of the sand wedge, and I took the club up with a little cock

of the right hand and then sliced it across and under the ball. The ball came out very high and softly.

I had wanted to hit it far enough to land it on the fringe, and it carried a little farther than I'd planned. It landed just on the green, took two short bounces and started to roll like a putt and break to the right.

When the ball was about five feet from the hole I started moving to my left to get a better view. When it was about a foot away I knew it was dead center and at that instant I knew I had a one-shot lead in the U.S. Open Championship.

I danced almost into the Pacific, then turned and pointed at Bruce and yelled, "I told you!"

Then my attention immediately shifted to the next hole.

No. 17

No. 18, 548 yards, par 5

This is the only hole where I altered my game plan. It's a position hole off the tee and also on the second shot. (I almost never go for it in two here, with the ocean in play from tee to green on the left.)

I drove with a 3-wood, aiming between the two trees on the right side of the fairway and drawing the ball. The ball skirted the left edge of the inside tree and bounced past it, and I was in good shape in the fairway, about 265 yards off the tee.

I usually lay up with a 5-iron, but went with a 7-iron instead. With the 5-iron I would have been hitting into a narrower part of the fairway. If you hit it to the right, there's a good chance a tree will block your third shot. If you hit it to the left, the ground slopes that way and the ball can kick into the rough, or worse yet into the bunker guarding the seawall. That had happened to me before. Also, *I had hit two poor partial wedge shots Sunday, and I wanted a full 9-iron into the green, or at least a full wedge.*

I hit the 7-iron farther than I expected to, about 160 yards, and I had 115 or 116 to the hole, into a slight wind. I made a nice, crisp swing with the 9-iron, and the ball started a little right of the flagstick and just stayed there, finishing about 20 feet past the hole.

I had a downhill, left-to-right putt, and I knew it was faster than lightning. All I wanted to do was lag it down and get it close. It was so fast, my only thought was to try to leave it three feet short.

When I hit the putt I thought the speed was good, but when it was halfway to the hole I thought I'd hit it too hard…if it missed the hole it was going to be four feet past. Then when it was four feet from the hole I thought it had a good chance to go in, and when it was two feet away it hit me that I had won. The feeling was all-consuming. I'd done it; I'd won the tournament I'd always wanted to win. I'd had a little magic in me, and I was the National Open Champion.

When to Be Aggressive
(and When Not to Be)

I'm sure you noticed in my recounting of my final nine holes at Pebble Beach that I played safely at certain times and aggressively at other times. I am basically an aggressive player—but I'll play safely when the potential penalty is too great and I'm in a position to win a tournament. If I have to make up strokes I'll take more risks, try to play closer to the pin on more difficult shots.

I'll also play safely or more dangerously depending on how I feel that particular day. If I'm playing well, I'll go at every flag. If I'm not playing very well and, say, I'm missing shots to the right, I won't aim directly at the pin or try to get too close to a pin that's tucked on the right part of the green. I'll play for the center of the green or the left center of the green, and if I do miss the shot right, I'll end up near the hole. If I hit the shot I'm playing, it'll be left of the hole but still on the green.

A very simple case of playing safely came in the 1983 British Open when I had to two-putt from 18 feet to win. Surveying the putt, I found it was fairly straight, but the last part was a little downhill. If I was too aggressive I could easily knock it three feet past the hole, so my only thought was to lag it up, and I left it just short of the hole for a tap-in. That was a time when I didn't want to get aggressive at all.

Chipping the ball, I'm usually pretty aggressive. I always try to get the ball to the pin, but there are times I will tell amateur players their best possible shot will put them 25 feet from the hole, or I tell them that just to get the ball on the green is a good shot. From a buried bunker lie or a bad lie in the rough around the green, that's often true.

In match play, which most people play, I have to use different strategy than when I play medal play, where every shot counts. Many times in match play, the play of my opponent tells me when to be aggressive and when not to be. If he's in trouble, I play safely. If I'm in trouble, I play more aggressively.

A final word

It is my hope that by reading this book you will develop a better short game, score lower and enjoy this wonderful game even more. Remember, not even the best players in the world hit all the greens in regulation.